Ang Lee: Interviews

Conversations with Filmmakers Series
Gerald Peary, General Editor

Ang Lee

INTERVIEWS

Edited by Karla Rae Fuller

University Press of Mississippi / Jackson

www.upress.state.ms.us

The University Press of Mississippi is a member
of the Association of American University Presses.

Copyright © 2016 by University Press of Mississippi
All rights reserved
Manufactured in the United States of America

First printing 2016

Library of Congress Control Number: 2015955714

Contents

Introduction

Ang Lee is one of the most diverse, versatile, and daring directors. He is the only Asian and nonwhite to win a Best Director Academy Award twice, once for *Brokeback Mountain* (2005) and once for *Life of Pi* (2012) up to this point. However, his contribution to cinema, his body of work, defies easy categorization, and many of the interviews in this volume explore the tension between his Taiwanese and Western film output.

First, though, a bit of background on Ang Lee to aid in our understanding of what makes him the unique filmmaker that he is. His father was a principal at one of the best high schools in Taiwan. Lee grew up watching lots of movies, but stated that he was brought up "non-artistically." He notes, "the idea in my family, in the culture itself, was to study something practical, get into a good college, then come to America and study, get a degree."[1] But he failed his college examinations and afterward went to the Academy of Art in Taiwan, majoring in theater and film. He did a lot of theater and then came Stateside to attend the University of Illinois at Champagne–Urbana. However, Lee's tenuous command of the language became a barrier in the States and he thus moved from acting to directing. He had already made two Super-8 films at the Taiwan Academy and that's how he was admitted into the New York University graduate filmmaking program. His thesis film, at forty-three minutes long, is entitled *Fine Line* and depicts an illegal female Chinese worker running from the immigration authorities and an Italian running from the mob. He got married in the summer of 1983 and finished his thesis film in 1984. Lee actually planned to return to Taiwan at that point, but his thesis film won Best Picture and Best Director at NYU. His wife got a job as a microbiologist and they moved to New York. Subsequently, he got an agent, but then spent the next six years in what he calls "development hell."

Lee's first feature turned out to be *Pushing Hands* (1992), which was originally written for a Taiwanese script competition. He didn't necessarily want to make it, but did want the $16,000 prize money. Lee had the idea for the film for two years: "It was set in a suburban house. In this house was an old man practicing T'ai Chi. So there's a lot of Chinese culture stuck in this house. The other half is an American wife who's a writer, very neurotic. So there's a split and in between they had a son who was between the old and new Chinese culture in America."[2] It took less than two months to write. The budget was $400,000. Lee met collaborators Ted Hope and James Schamus of Good Machine production company who helped get the film made. His meeting with his producers was somewhat humorous, but ended the drought of lack of filmmaking opportunity: "I pitched the story to them, and James said to me, 'No wonder you couldn't get anything made for six years. You're the worst pitcher—you can't pitch your way out of a basket.' They pitched themselves to me as the kings of no-budget filmmaking. Not low-budget, no budget. So we hooked up."[3]

The shoot was very stressful with twelve-to-sixteen-hour days, Lee's wife's sickness after the birth of their second son, and his resulting lack of sleep throughout. For Lee, time is the main enemy on independent films because he never gets as many shots he plans on. In spite of this, Lee was very much hands-on in post-production as he literally sat beside the editor and participated in every cut.

The theme of the movie is about change in society. *Pushing Hands* is essentially about the conflicts that arise when an elderly Chinese tai chi master (played by Sihung Lung) comes to the United States to live with his son and American daughter-in-law. For a Chinese person it's about becoming a Westerner. According to Lee, the Eastern way is that everybody tries to diminish differences—there's tolerance, acceptance until finally things explode. It's a big shock, chaos, and then people find new lives and a new balance. There is also an importance of filial piety. In Lee's words, you become a Westerner and betray your parents with total guilt.

Pushing Hands was embraced in Taiwan but not elsewhere. In the film, Lee has his characters spend lots of time in the kitchen. One of his favorite places to shoot is the kitchen because it's both a battlefield and personal with different levels of interaction. The first fifteen to twenty minutes has no dialogue; language differences between characters play a key role to communication or miscommunication, so the absence of language gives the audience a bit of peace or, perhaps more appropriately, the calm before the storm.

The film is about an old man who explores whether or not a person is loyal and expresses filial piety toward their parents, despite the fact that Lee initially didn't want to make what he considered to be old-fashioned films, "the kind that people had already stopped making when I was little."[4] *Pushing Hands* begins Lee's trio of features completed by *The Wedding Banquet* produced the following year and *Eat Drink Man Woman* the year after. These three films in retrospect became known as Lee's "Father Knows Best" trilogy due to each feature's emphasis on the relationship between a father and his children. Lee has admitted that many of the conflicts at play between the character of the father and his offspring mirror those between himself and his own father.

Lee's second feature, *The Wedding Banquet*, also depicted a tense relationship of the main character, a gay Taiwanese American man, Wai-Tung, who has been hiding his live-in relationship with another man, Simon, from both his parents. A Taiwanese studio funded *The Wedding Banquet* for $750,000. James Schamus at that point offered to help Lee with the script, and according to Lee a long-term collaboration was born. In the filmmaker's words, because Schamus did help with the script, "the rest, I would like to say, is history."[5] The story of *The Wedding Banquet* takes off when Wai-Tung tries to please his parents through a "marriage of convenience" to a Mainland Chinese immigrant woman, Wei-Wei, who is desperate for legal status. *The Wedding Banquet*'s "mix of drama, comedy, and cultural critique" made it both a commercial and critical success with Oscar and Golden Globe nominations, a Golden Bear award at the Berlin Film Festival, and a sweep at the Golden Horse Awards, with six major prizes.[6]

In the film *The Wedding Banquet*, it could be said that there are as many as five main characters: Wai-Tung, his gay lover Simon, his legal wife Wei-Wei, his mother, and his father (again played by Sihung Lung): "At the beginning of the film, it seems that this will be Wai-Tung's story, but as the film goes on, the other characters are given screen-time and back-story in almost equal amounts. The narrative reflects how powerfully decisions in the film impact upon the five-member family unit as a whole."[7] James Schamus, a co-producer, describes the storyline "as following the arc of a typical 1930s Hollywood screwball comedy—except that it was gay and Chinese!"[8] Lee goes on to say that "each of the five main characters represents the extreme of something, and you put them together and observe what happens."[9] The director also admits that he has always had "identity problems" stemming from generational geographical displacement. "He [Wai-Tung] is united with the motherland of China through this woman [Wei-Wei], and then the parents come in. It is on one level a political satire, China and Taiwan united, with the influence of America in the middle trying to bring them together. It just naturally came out that way."[10]

In an interview with Lee conducted by Chris Berry for *Metro Magazine* in 1994, Lee talks about the kissing scene between Wai-Tung and Simon being a first for the Taiwanese cinema at the time. But along with that cultural shock came the rather retrograde reality of a sentiment of being Chinese in New York. For example, you might be from Mainland China, Hong Kong, or Taiwan, but in New York, you're just Chinese. Lee discusses the different response by different audiences internationally— especially the Taiwanese and American ones. The two Chinas coming together through the characters of Wai-Tung and Wei-Wei gets laughs in Taipei, while the language of the New York marriage bureau gets laughs in the States.

Eat Drink Man Woman (1994), Lee's third feature, depicts the relationship between a widower ex-chef father (played again by Sihung Lung) and his three single daughters. Lee returned to Taiwan to make this film that can be said to be "a celebration of food and love (both familial and romantic)" [11]: "Mr. Chu has three very different daughters, all of whom find their matches in the end, and he must get past the attentions of a scheming, overbearing woman in order to find his own romantic happiness. In this accessible and familiar format, Ang once again explored his pet themes of fatherhood, family, and duty."[12]

Even if considered part of his "Father Knows Best" trilogy, Lee feels that he began to depart from what he had done in his first two features in some significant ways: "I was beginning to experiment with cinema and was thinking mostly of cubism. Instead of a linear structure, I was looking at a different way to hold the movie. So I was trying to develop one incident or one character and look at it from all sides. But when you want to watch from all sides, you also have to shoot in a way that reflects that."[13]

Eat Drink Man Woman takes place in Taiwan, and Lee has noted the influences of Japanese director Yasujiro Ozu and other Chinese family dramas as influences. But he actually mentions a Chinese saying that most inspired him in relation to this film, "All banquets must eventually come to an end."[14] Food is certainly a metaphor, but Lee feels that the banquet is really the important element representing how he felt about his home country of Taiwan. The film was nominated for an Oscar for Best Foreign Language Film (like the previous *The Wedding Banquet*) and was a major critical success. It was also a commercial success, becoming the most successful Chinese-language film ever to be released in the United States up to that point.

Clearly, the focus on human relationships at the heart of Lee's work uniquely prepared him for a seemingly very different project, directing a version of Jane Austen's *Sense and Sensibility* (1995). A number of critics felt that this adaptation was a natural transition from *Eat Drink Man Woman*, which was often characterized as a comedy of manners. The film's writer-star Emma Thompson was also impressed by Lee's prior work and noted that "working with Ang had taught her that the whole is greater than the sum of the parts."[15]

Sense and Sensibility was technically Lee's first all-English-language film, and the director felt that he received enormous support particularly from Thompson and the production designer. Lee describes about six months of research prior to shooting where he learned whatever he could from reading literature, visiting museums and houses, landscape scouting, and looking at costumes oftentimes with lead actress Emma Thompson in tow.[16] Lee admits that it was a long learning process and that Thompson was very generous about taking him "to museums to go through paintings from that particular time so I could see the spirit of romanticism coming up, the rise of metropolitanism and the industrial revolution."[17] Indeed, Lee was often asked how he was able to make the leap to a culture and a time so different from his own: "A lot of people ask, 'How did you do that?' But I didn't do it overnight by myself! I was a whole team of people, and they used my heart and cinematic talent through that collaboration. It was a group effort. After a period of time, I almost forgot that I am a Chinese doing this. To me, I don't divide my work between Chinese film and American film."[18]

In *Sense and Sensibility*, the core of the narrative centers around two sisters, Elinor (played by Emma Thompson) and Marianne (played by Kate Winslet) and how they each embody sense and sensibility. Elinor is more sense and Marianne more sensibility. Despite settings in seemingly despite two very different cultures and time periods, there is the same line in both *Eat Drink Man Woman* and *Sense and Sensibility* when one sister says to the other, "What do you know of my heart?"[19]

Though Lee had a few struggles with the British cast's way of working, the film earned rave reviews and was nominated for seven Academy Awards, including Best Picture. Lee was not nominated in the Best Director category, but Emma Thompson's screenplay did win an Oscar. Lee considered this a "good transition" film for himself professionally as it was an A-list production,

Lee's next film was *The Ice Storm* (1997), his first fully American film based on the 1994 novel of the same name by Rick Moody. Set during the Thanksgiving holiday in 1973, *The Ice Storm* is about two essentially dysfunctional families in the wealthy enclave of New Canaan, Connecticut, each of whom are trying to deal with the political and social changes of the early 1970s. Their escape through alcohol, adultery, and sexual experimentation indirectly leads to tragic results.

Lee's producing partners, James Schamus and Ted Hope, who had worked with him on *The Wedding Banquet* and *Eat Drink Man Woman*, were looking for more English-language material for him to direct. After Lee read the novel by Rick Moody, he felt that it was "wonderfully cinematic material."[20] However, Lee rushed the production that was supposed to take place during fall and winter into a spring and summer shooting schedule. Lee rationalizes his motivation as having to do with the overwhelmingly positive reception of *Sense and Sensibility*: "The whole success and all the publicity around *Sense and Sensibility* made me very jaded and I just couldn't wait to get back to work, so we just went ahead."[21] Not only was the production hindered by attempts to mask the seasons, but also some of the residents from the New Canaan area that the film depicts objected to the filming due to the novel's "unfavorable" references to drugs and wife-swapping.[22]

Though the film features an ensemble cast of Kevin Kline, Joan Allen, Tobey Maguire, Christina Ricci, Elijah Wood, and Sigourney Weaver, *The Ice Storm* only grossed $8 million on a budget of around $18 million. In the end, *The Ice Storm*, though critically well received, was not a commercial success and lost money. Lee contends that the studio did not support a strong release or work with him throughout the distribution process. He says that the company did not even let him know when the DVD was going to be released. However, *The Ice Storm* has done well with DVD sales and in ancillary markets such as cable so that there is a higher awareness of the film over time.

Ride with the Devil (1999), Lee's next feature, represents a complete departure from the "family dramas" that are at the heart of each of his films from *Pushing Hands* to *The Ice Storm*. Set during the Civil War, the storyline was conceived from a screenplay written by James Schamus, based on a book entitled *Woe to Live On*, by author Daniel Woodrell. The events depicted in the film focus on the escalating guerilla warfare of a Southern militia group against Union soldiers in Missouri at the onset of the war. The ensemble cast features Tobey Maguire, Skeet Ulrich, Jeffrey Wright, Jonathan Brandis, Jim Caviezel, and musician Jewel.

One of the most memorable elements of *Ride with the Devil* is the role of Holt, played by Jeffrey Wright, a freed slave who fights on the side of the Confederacy because of his loyalty to a Southern friend. In the film, Holt's character does not speak for the first twenty to thirty minutes of the film. He is an important if temporarily mute presence. It seems risky, but we have seen before in Lee's first feature *Pushing Hands* that this director is willing to insert and perhaps relishes non-verbal sequences that can last over twenty minutes. In fact, Lee has stated that he prefers scenes and dramatic moments where the characters do not speak with dialogue, but rather through body language and blocking.

Issues of identity also abound in this film. Southern militiaman Jake Roedel (played by Tobey Maguire) is German born and his family has sided with the Union soldiers. He is an outsider among the band of Southerners. As such, he and Holt form a formidable bond as outsiders who understand what it means to be conflicted in terms of regional, national, and racial identity. In *Ride with the Devil*, Lee goes outside of his comfort zone of family dramas to take on the epic nature of the broader allegiances and alliances of the Civil War.

Unfortunately, *Ride with the Devil* was given a very limited theatrical released and "dumped" according to Lee. It is an unusual film, violent, though not cathartically so, full of odd characters who do a lot of talking (notably, in the dialect of the time period) with a plot that could be described as meandering. However, this film represents a departure for Lee and the types of family-centered films he was associated with. He felt that he could handle "bigger" movies after this initial attempt.

Indeed, in *Crouching Tiger, Hidden Dragon* (2000), Lee handles a "big" movie with an international cast. Much has been written about this film, its characters, the high quality of the martial arts sequences and also more controversially, the cultural/language differences and backgrounds of the main cast members. First and foremost, *Crouching Tiger, Hidden Dragon* is a love story between characters Li Mu Bai (played by Chow Yun-Fat) and Yu Shu Lien (played by Michelle Yeoh). Supporting characters include Jen (played by Zhang Ziyi), Jade Fox (played by Cheng Pei-pei) and Jen's bandit lover, Lo (played by Chang Chen). The plot is filled with divided loyalties, couplings and uncouplings, teacher and student dynamics, and female desire for adventure and mastery while peppered with jaw dropping martial arts sequences.

Crouching Tiger, Hidden Dragon comes from the fourth part of a five-part novel by Wang Dulu and the title refers to "something else that may be going on under a proper societal surface."[23] Lee has stated his admiration for the author of the novel: "I always liked this writer and the old-fashioned, nostalgic way he approached classic Chinese culture. There is a degree of realism to his work—it doesn't go too crazy, too out of bounds. It has outstanding female characters and it has a tragic ending, both of which are unusual for a martial arts story."[24]

He has further explained how the novel is what is known as a "wuxia tale." "'Wu' means military, martial. 'Xia' means the knight, the rightful warrior."[25] However, s/he is different from the samurai or knight-errant because a wuxia is not a class, it's not a job:[26] "A 'warrior with righteousness' is what it is, but free in style. They're more like the Western movie loner, than the samurai-type knight-errant, who works for the government, the church. Wanderers, drifters. In the book, both Li Mu Bai, and the woman Yu Shu Lien, are of the wuxia."[27]

In an interview with James Schamus, Lee relates that it was both rewarding and challenging to write a script together (with Schamus) that resulted in a film with a more global appeal, a factor that also dictated the decision to make the film in Chinese as opposed to two versions— one English and one Chinese as once proposed.[28]

With the significant contribution of fight choreographer Yuen Woo-Ping, *Crouching Tiger, Hidden Dragon* became a surprise international hit, grossing over $200 million. It grossed over $100 million in the United States, becoming the highest-grossing foreign language film in American history. The film won the Academy Award for Best Foreign Language Film (Taiwan) and three other Academy Awards, and was nominated for six other Academy Awards, including Best Picture.

An even larger-scale project, *Hulk* (2003), surpassed all of Lee's previous films in terms of budget and scale with the added element of special effects. Lee admittedly did not grow up as a comic book fan, but did try to add "heart and complexity" to what could have been just another typical summer blockbuster.[29] The film stars relative newcomer Eric Bana (as Dr. Bruce Banner/the Hulk), as well as Jennifer Connelly (his love interest, Betty), Sam Elliot (as her father), Josh Lucas, and Nick Nolte (as Bruce's father, scientist David Banner). Though this film was Lee's largest-scale effort thus far, the director seemed to return to the family drama, albeit on an epic scale, particularly in the exploration of the relationship between Bruce Banner and his father, David.

Clearly Lee got the chance to do *Hulk*, his first big-studio blockbuster, on the strength of his startling success with *Crouching Tiger, Hidden Dragon*. Lee talked about how he had something to prove, namely to himself: "I wanted to do it all. I wanted a movie that satisfied the audience desire for action. But I also wanted to establish . . . a psycho-drama, a kind of emotional intensity that drives the action along. And that process brings with it some conflict and controversy. But the challenge got me excited. I wanted to prove to myself that I could do it."[30]

Lee integrated crowd-pleasing action with intense psychodrama. The Hulk is afraid of being out of control of his Hulk alter ego and yet also strangely liberated by the destructive Hulk episode, reflecting a common theme in Lee's work, the issue of emotional repression. It exists in some form or another in every one of his films. Ultimately, his episodes as the Hulk isolate him from his love interest Betty and make him the object of terror for the government and exploitation from private interests. However, the major conflict does not culminate in a fight with a mighty villain as is the tradition in most superhero/comic book films. Rather it is his father's unintended transfer of radiation that makes Bruce the Hulk that provides the focus of a climactic faceoff at the end of the film.

Despite over two years of work—with Lee even donning the Hulk suit to provide the movement for the computer generated images—the film received disappointing reviews. The film didn't seem to resonate strongly with comic book fans (even with the occasional split-screen comic-book-styled visuals) who found changes in the origin story and the special effects problematic. However, some critics appreciated Lee's attempt to portray the tortured relationship between Bruce and his father David Banner and were impressed by the added psychological depth not usually accorded to most blockbusters with comic book origins.

Lee regrouped and decided to scale back to a smaller, more intimate dimension for his next film project with overwhelmingly positive success. *Brokeback Mountain* (2005) depicts the twenty-odd-year romantic and sexual relationship between two cowboys, Ennis Del Mar (played by Heath Ledger) and Jack Twist (played by Jake Gyllenhaal).

The film is based on a short story written by E. Annie Proulx published in the *New Yorker* in 1997. This groundbreaking project had a long history before director Ang Lee signed on to direct it: "For . . . seven years, the project kicked around Hollywood—it was at one time attached to Joel Schumacher and at another to Gus Van Sant—where it gathered dust as well as admiration as one of the great unproduced screenplays. Eventually, Lee, coming off the exhaustion of having done two complicated action pictures, remembered it and got producer James Schamus and Focus Features, which Schamus is co-president of, on board."[31]

Lee is very forthcoming about his response to the short story and the script. He says that he cried and that he was deeply moved by the story. He has said that he attempts to find the universal in stories about outsiders. He attributes his ability to relate to his outsider characters is that he, too, feels like a perpetual outsider. Leaving his native Taiwan, relocating to a different country left him feeling fully a part of neither, thus, he maintains that he has this unique perspective, that of an outside observer where conventions that most assume to be a given are consistently challenged.

With *The Wedding Banquet* and *Brokeback Mountain*, Lee started to acquire a reputation of a straight director who makes some of the best gay films. Lee, however, considers *Brokeback Mountain* primarily a universally relatable love story whether you're gay or straight.[32]

The setting is critical to the dramatic power of the film. For Lee, Brokeback Mountain had to be a character because the ideas at work in the film are so abstract. Lee summarizes this succinctly: "It is a very existential idea to me. It's about the illusion of love. They keep wanting to go back to something they really didn't understand to begin with, when they are inside of it. They never get it. And when they get it, they've missed it. I think that is the theme for me that got me hooked."[33]

Brokeback Mountain represents a creative and, according to the director, personal resurrection. Lee describes the experience of making *Brokeback Mountain* in several publications as "healing" from the grueling experience in the production of *Hulk* and the mixed response the film ultimately received. Lee received the Academy Award for Best Director for this film, though it lost Best Picture to the film *Crash*—a decidedly controversial result for many who were hoping that *Brokeback Mountain* would win.

The film *Lust, Caution* (2007) marks a return to China for Lee. This film is an espionage thriller based on the novella of the same name published in 1979 by Chinese author Eileen Chang. It depicts a group of university students who plot to assassinate a high-ranking special agent and recruiter of the puppet government using an attractive young woman to lure him into a trap.

The film contains scenes of graphic sexuality that are both passionate and sado-masochistic, and Lee explains how the scenes create a narrative of their own: "The sex scenes have to tell a story. They have to work in such a way that the body language tells you something. There's a dramatic purpose in those scenes. Wong needs to fall in love, so we have the scene where Mr. Yee is cuddling her, and she's in the foetus position. He seems to squeeze the life out of her, and yet she is moved."[34]

Indeed, Lee compares his direction of the sex scenes with that of "a choreographer in a martial arts film." He states that most of the sexual positions between the two leading actors were created with a clear dramatic purpose. He would find the body language that would "say most explicitly what I needed to say" and then go through it with the actors. He'd talk about the "drama of the scene, what was going through their minds and how they'd give and take."[35]

Lee felt *Lust, Caution* to be an extremely personal film, not only because it's in the Chinese language, but more so because of the process of directing the characters in the movie "with my personal knowledge with feelings and things inside of me that I'm not aware of."[36] *Lust, Caution* won the Golden Lion at the Venice Film Festival, the second award for Lee as he had won it the year before for *Brokeback Mountain*. He refused to make any changes in the film to attempt to get an R rating theatrically, though the DVD was edited for an R-rating release so that it would be more widely available in rental outlets and stores.[37]

Taking Woodstock (2009) is the relatively light-hearted follow-up to the very intense *Lust, Caution*. *Taking Woodstock* is based on the true story of Eliot Tiber (played by Demetri Martin), who along with his parents, owners of a dilapidated motel in upstate New York (played by Henry Goodman and Imelda Staunton), find themselves at the center of the cultural happening of the Woodstock music concert in 1969. However, Lee made clear that *Taking Woodstock* is not a movie about music, but is instead essentially a study of familial relationships, admittedly familiar ground for the director.

Lee was drawn to the idea of directing a comedy after the controversy surrounding *Lust, Caution*. He describes not being able to sleep and breaking into uncontrollable weeping at unexpected moments after the tremendous emotional and physical toll of both the production and promotion of the Chinese-language film in both Asia and the United States.[38]

Taking Woodstock took forty-two days to shoot and about $30 million to produce, almost twice the budget of *Lust, Caution*. It only grossed a fraction of its budget. Some audiences expected a documentary, a concert film, or a perhaps a more provocative gay coming-out film. Many seemed disappointed despite some positive reviews for Lee's unique take on this specifically American watershed cultural moment.

Lee's next film is widely regarded as a technological as well as artistic triumph. *Life of Pi* (2012), a 3D live-action and computer-generated adventure drama is based on Yann Martel's 2001 novel of the same name:

"The storyline revolves around an Indian man named Piscine Molitor 'Pi' Patel, living in Canada and telling a novelist about his life story and how at sixteen he survives a shipwreck in which his family dies, and is stranded in the Pacific Ocean on a lifeboat with a Bengal tiger named Richard Parker."[39] Thought to be "unfilmable," *Life of Pi* as a film project had been in different hands for many years. Other directors, including M. Night Shyamalan and Alfonso Cuaron, had considered and rejected the complex story since Fox acquired the film rights in 2003.[40] Lee spent four years on the project and almost immediately decided that it should be in 3D,[41] as he felt that the many scenes on the lifeboat with the tiger would need some sort of visual amplification to keep the audience's interest.

However, even after Lee signed on to the project, there were times when he didn't think it would actually get made. He shared with journalists that this was really the only time in his career that he felt this way: "It was right before we started the physical pre-production. I previsualized the whole ocean part before we made the movie, I was that prepared. At one point they seemed to want to drop it because it was really risky . . . but once I get on something I have to finish it; I just kept persuading them and they turned around."[42]

Not only is *Life of Pi* a feast for the eyes and for the heart, but also for the mind. The film concludes with "a fascinating, deliberately prosaic coda that raises questions about the reality of what we've seen."[43] The audience is asked to believe in the unbelievable, and the film melds the fantastic technological wizardry of a blockbuster with the deeper questions and universal issues of an art film. *Life of Pi* emerged as a critical and commercial success, earning over $600 million worldwide, nearly six times its budget. It was nominated for eleven Academy Awards and won four: Best Original Score, Best Visual Effects, Best Cinematography, and Best Director for Lee.

Lee has been coined a "versatile," "genre hopping," "genre shifting," and "diverse" filmmaker given his seemingly eclectic choices of subject matter and visual treatment in his prior films. In terms of Lee's distinctive approach and his passion for filmmaking, the director describes it best: "Whatever material excites me, they'll call for a certain genre or combination of genres. It'll come naturally and I'll be eager to learn how that thing works. I learn the rules, and I'll probably break some of them. You have to know the rules, otherwise you have no tools to communicate to the audience, but to keep it fresh you have to break some. I don't choose genres as the element, but the material itself is the element, then

I'll decide what genre I need. That's just how I work."[44] Well said, by a formidable filmmaker who has shown that he creates without limits, without labels, and without fear.

KRF

Notes

1. Glenn Kenny, "Crossing Borders," *DGA Quarterly* 4, no. 1 (Spring 2010).

2. Stephen Lowenstein, ed., "Ang Lee: *Pushing Hands*," in *My First Movie* (New York: Penguin Books, 2002), 368.

3. Kenny.

4. Michael Berry, ed., "Ang Lee: Freedom in Film," in *Speaking in Images: Interviews with Contemporary Chinese Filmmakers* (New York: Columbia University Press, 2005), 331.

5. Kenny.

6. Berry, 326.

7. Whitney Crothers Dilley, *The Cinema of Ang Lee: The Other Side of the Screen* (London and New York: Wallflower Press, 2007), 62.

8. Dilley, 61.

9. Berry, 331.

10. Berry, 332.

11. Nick Dawson, "Father Knows Best: The Early Comedies of Ang Lee," www.focusfeatures.com, June 19, 2009.

12. Dawson.

13. Berry, 337.

14. Berry, 336.

15. Dawson.

16. Berry, 338.

17. Berry, 338.

18. Berry, 338.

19. Dilley, 88.

20. Iain Blair, "Ang Lee: The Director Braves *The Ice Storm* in His New Fox Searchlight Release," *Film & Video*, October 1997, 50.

21. Blair, 50.

22. Blair, 50.

23. Mitch Persons, "Ang Lee on *Crouching Tiger, Hidden Dragon*," *Cinefantastique*, 33, no. 1/2 (April 2001): 96.

24. Persons, 96–97.

25. Persons, 97.

26. Persons, 97.

27. Persons, 97.

28. "Ang Lee and James Schamus," guardian.co.uk, November 2000.

29. Ian Grey, "An Even More Incredible Hulk," www.fangoria.com, June 2003.

30. Gene Seymour, "Aarrgh!! Another Leap for Ang Lee," *Newsday*, June 15, 2003.

31. Peter Bowen, "Ride the High Country," *Filmmaker*, October 1, 2005, 34.

32. Garth Franklin, "Interview: Ang Lee, *Brokeback Mountain*," *Dark Horizons*, www
.darkhorizons.com, December 2005.

33. Carlo Cavagna, "Interview of Ang Lee", www.Aboutfilm.com, December 2005.

34. Damon Wise, "Censor Sensibility," *Empire*, December 2007, 167.

35. Wise, 167.

36. Jennifer Merin, "Taking What He Gives," *New York Press*, September 2007, 27.

37. Wikipedia.org/Lust, Caution (film).

38. Damon Wise, "Hippie Talking," www.empireonline.com, November 2009.

39. Wikipedia.org/Life of Pi (film).

40. John Hiscock, "Ang Lee, Interview: How He Filmed the Unfilmable for *Life of Pi*,"
www.telegraph.co.uk, December 19, 2012.

41. Hiscock.

42. Steve "Frosty" Weintraub, "Ang Lee Talks *Life of Pi*, the Difficulty of Getting the
Project Off the Ground, 3D as a New Artistic Form, Deleted Scenes and More," www
.collider.com, October 3, 2012.

43. Philip French, "*Life of Pi*—Review," www.theguardian.com, December 23, 2012.

44. Weintraub.

Chronology

1954   Born on October 23 in the town of Chaochou in Pingtung, Taiwan.

1971   Graduates from National Tainan First Senior High School.

1973   Enrolls in National Taiwan University of Arts in Taipei as a drama student.

1975   Graduates from the National Taiwan University of Arts.

1976   Serves two-year term in the military in Taiwan.

1978   Leaves Taiwan to attend the University of Illinois, Urbana-Champaign; subsequently receives BFA in theater.

1980   Attends New York University. *The Runner*, student short.

1981   *I Love Chinese Food*, student short.

1982   *I Wish I Was By That Dim Lake*, student short.

1983   Marries Jane Lin.

1984   Acts as assistant cameraman on Spike Lee NYU thesis film, *Joe's Bed-Stuy Barbershop: We Cut Heads*. His son Haan is born.

1986   Directs *Fine Line*, MFA thesis film at NYU. For the next six years he is unemployed. Works as a house-husband, taking care of his children.

1990   His son Mason is born.

1992   Directs *Pushing Hands*. Director, editor, producer, and screenwriter

1993   Directs *The Wedding Banquet*. Director, producer, screenwriter, and cameo appearance.

1994   Directs *Eat Drink Man Woman*. Director and screenwriter.

1995   Directs *Sense and Sensibility*. Co-produces and co-writes *Siao Yu* directed by Sylvia Chang.

1997   Directs *The Ice Storm*. Director and producer.

1999   Directs *Ride With the Devil*.

2000   Directs *Crouching Tiger, Hidden Dragon*. Director and producer.

2001   Wins Academy Award for Best Foreign Language Film for *Crouching Tiger, Hidden Dragon*. Directs *Chosen* (from the BMW compilation of short films, *The Hire*). Wins Golden Globe for *Crouching Tiger, Hidden Dragon*

2003   Directs *Hulk*.

2005   Directs *Brokeback Mountain*.

2006   Wins Academy Award for Best Director for *Brokeback Mountain*—the first person of Asian heritage and the first non-white person to do so.

2007   Directs *Lust, Caution*. Wins the Golden Lion at the Venice Film Festival. Appears as interviewee in the documentary *Hollywood Chinese*.

2009   Directs *Taking Woodstock*.

2012   Directs *Life of Pi*. Director and producer.

2013   Wins second Academy Award for Best Director for *Life of Pi*.

Filmography

I WISH I WAS BY THAT DIM LAKE (SHORT) (1982)
Director: **Ang Lee**
Screenplay: **Ang Lee**
32 minutes

PUSHING HANDS (1992)
Director: **Ang Lee**
Screenplay: **Ang Lee**, James Schamus
Producers: **Ang Lee**, James Schamus, Sui Je Cheng, Ted Hope, Li-Kong
    Hsu, Feng-Chyt Jiang
Camera: Lin Jong
Editing: **Ang Lee**, Tim Squyres
Set Design: Scott Bradley
Music: Xiao-Song Qu
Cast: Sihung Lung, Lai Wang, Bo Z. Wang, Deb Snyder, Fanny De Luz,
    Haan Lee, Hung-Chang Wang, Jeanne Kuo Chang, James Lou
105 minutes

THE WEDDING BANQUET (1993)
Director: **Ang Lee**
Screenplay: **Ang Lee**, Neil Peng, James Schamus
Producers: Sui Le Cheng, Dolly Hall, Ted Hope, Li-Kong Hsu, Feng-Chyt
    Jiang, **Ang Lee**, James Schamus
Camera: Lin Jong
Editing: Tim Squyres
Set Design: Steve Rosenzweig
Music: Mader
Cast: Yai-lei Kuei, Sihung Lung, May Chin, Winston Chao, Mitchell Li-
    chtenstein, Dion Birney, Jeanne Kuo Chang, Paul Chen, Chung-Wei
    Chou, Yun Chung, Ho-Mean Fu, Michael Gaston, Jeffrey Howard,
    Theresa Hou, Yung-The Hsu, Jean Hu, Albert Huang, Neal Huff,

Anthony Ingoglia, Eddie Johns, Thomas Koo, Chih Kuan, Robert Larenquent, Neal Lee, Mason Lee, Dean Li, Jennifer Lin, John Nathan, Francis Pan, Neal Peng, Tien Pein, Marny Pocato, Tonia Rowe, Chung-Hsien Su, Hannah Sullivan, Elizabeth Yang, Vanessa Yang, Wei-Huang Ying, Peide Yao

106 minutes

EAT DRINK MAN WOMAN (1994)

Director: **Ang Lee**

Screenplay: **Ang Lee**, James Schamus, Hui-Ling Wang

Producers: Ted Hope, Kong Hsu, Li-Kong Hsu, Feng-Chyt Jiang, James Schamus

Camera: Lin Jong

Editing: Tim Squyres

Set Design: Fu-Hsiung Lee

Music: Mader

Cast: Sihung Lung, Yu-Wen Wang, Chien-lien Wu, Kuei-Mei Yang, Sylvia Chang, Winston Chao, Chao-jung Chen, Chit-man Chan, Yu Chen, Ya-lei Kuei, Chi-Der Hong, Gin-Ming Hsu, Huey-Yi Lin, Shih-Jay Lin, Chin-Cheng Lu, Cho-Gin Nei, Yu-Chien Tang, Chung Ting, Cheng-Fen Tso, Man-Sheng Tu, Chuen Wang, Shui Wang, Hwa Wu, Po-hsiung Wu, Michael Taylor

124 minutes

SENSE AND SENSIBILITY (1995)

Director: **Ang Lee**

Screenplay: Emma Thompson

Producers: Laurie Borg, Lindsay Doran, Sydney Pollack, James Schamus, Geoff Stier

Camera: Michael Coulter

Editing: Tim Squyres

Set Design: Luciana Arrighi

Music: Patrick Doyle

Cast: James Fleet, Tom Wilkinson, Harriet Walter, Kate Winslet, Emma Thompson, Gemma Jones, Hugh Grant, Emilie Francois, Elizabeth Spriggs, Robert Hardy, Ian Brimble, Isabelle Amyes, Alan Rickman, Greg Wise, Alexander John, Imelda Staunton, Imogen Stubbs, Hugh Laurie, Allan Mitchell, Josephine Gradwell, Richard Lumsden, Lone Vidahl, Oliver Ford Davies, Eleanor McCready, Lindsay Doran

136 minutes

SHAO NU XIAO YU (1995)
Director: Sylvia Chang
Screenplay: Sylvia Chang, **Ang Lee**, Geiling Yan
Producers: **Ang Lee**, Hu-Yan Chung, Dolly Hall, Li-Kong Hsu, Feng-
    Chyt Jiang
Camera: Joe DeSalvo
Editing: Feng Mei
Set Design: Wing Lee
Music: Bobbi Dar
Cast: Rene Liu, Marj Dusay, Chung-Hua Tou, Daniel J. Travanti, Tai-
    Feng Hsia, Jill Church, Ajay Mehta, Daxing Zhang
104 minutes

THE ICE STORM (1997)
Director: **Ang Lee**
Screenplay: James Schamus
Producers: Alysse Bezahler, Anthony Bregman, Ted Hope, **Ang Lee**,
    James Schamus
Camera: Fredrick Elmes
Editing: Tim Squyres
Set Design: Mark Friedberg
Music: Bill Brennan, Christopher Dedrick, Mark Duggan, Brad Haehnel,
    Daniel Cecil Hill, Jamie Hopkings, Pal Houle, Blair Mackay, Patrick
    Mullins, Alex Steyermark, Maisie Weissman, Ron Korb
Cast: Kevin Kline, Joan Allen, Sigourney Weaver, Henry Czerny, Tobey
    Maguire, Christina Ricci, Elijah Wood, Adam Hann-Byrd, David
    Krumholtz, Jamey Sheridan, Kate Burton, William Cain, Michael
    Cumpsty, Maia Danziger, Katie Holmes, Michael Egerman, Christine
    Farrell, Glenn Fitzgerald, Allison Janney, Jonathan Freeman, Bar-
    bara Garrick, Dennis Gagomiros, John Benjamin Hickey, Tom Flagg,
    Byron Jennings, Miles Marek, Colette Kilroy, Ivan Kronenfeld, Daniel
    McDonald, Donna Mitchell, Barbara Neal, Nancy Opel, Larry Pine,
    Wendy Scott, Marcell Rosenblatt, Evelyn Solann, Jessica Stone, Sarah
    Thompson, Scott Wentworth, Robert Westenberg
112 minutes

RIDE WITH THE DEVIL (1999)
Director: **Ang Lee**
Screenplay: Daniel Woodrell, James Schamus

Producers: Anne Carey, Robert F. Colesberry, Ted Hope, David Linde, James Schamus

Camera: Fredrick Elmes

Editing: Tim Squyres

Set Design: Mark Friedberg

Music: Michael Danna

Cast: Tobey Maguire, Jeremey W. Auman, Scott Sener, Skeet Ulrich, Glenn Q. Pierce, Kathleen Warfel, David Darlow, Zan McLeod, John Whelan, Roger Landes, Jeffrey Dover, Tyler Johnson, Kelly Werts, Michael W. Nash, John Judd, Don Shanks, Jay Thorson, Dean Vivian, Cheryl Weaver, Jim Caviezel, Jonathan Rhys Meyers, Simon Baker, Matthew Faber, Tom Guiry, Jonathan Brandis, Jeffrey Wright, Celia Wilson, Amber Griffith, Ric Averill, Buck Baker, Mark Ruffalo, Stephen Mailer, Zach Grenier, Donna Thompson, Cassie Mae Sears, Jewel Kilcher, Margo Martindale, Tom Wilkinson, Martin Liebschner Jr., Marvin Schroeder, Steven Price, David L. Asher, James Urbaniak, David Rees Snell, John Ales, Dave Wilson, Larry Greer, Kevin Fewell, Michel Owen, John Durbin, Jim Shelby, Addison Myers, Michael Linsley Rapport, Joseph Patrick Moynihan, Jennie Nauman, Christine Brandt, Bill Grivna, Nora Denney, Harry Gibbs, Clayton Vest, Roger Denesha, Jacob Kozlowski, David Lee Burnos Jr., Jennifer Ackland, T. Max Graham

138 minutes

CROUCHING TIGER, HIDDEN DRAGON (2000)

Director: **Ang Lee**

Screenplay: Hui-Ling Wang, James Schamus, Kuo Jang Tsai

Producers: Bo-Chu Chui, Ping Dong, Li-Kong Hsu, William Kong, **Ang Lee**, Philip Lee, David Linde, Er-Dong Liu, Kelly Miller, James Schamus, Wai Sum Shia, Quangang Zheng

Camera: Peter Pau

Editing: Tim Squyres

Set Design: Timmy Yip

Music: Dun Tan

Cast: Yun-Fat Chow, Michelle Yeoh, Ziyi Zhang, Chen Chang, Si-hung Lung, Pei-pei Cheng, Fa Zeng Li, Xian Gao, Yan Hai, De Ming Wang, Li Li, Su Ying Huang, Jin Ting Zhang, Rei Yang, Kai Li, Kian Hua Feng, Zhen Xi Du, Cheng Lin Xu, Feng Lin, Wen Sheng Wang, Dong Song, Zhong Xuan Ma, Bao Cheng Li, Yong De Yang, Shao

Jun Zhang, Ning Ma, Jian Min Zhu, Chang Cheng Don, Yi Shih, Bin
Chen, Sao Chen Chang
120 minutes

CHOSEN (2001) [short]
Director: **Ang Lee**
Screenplay: David Carter
Producers: Robyn Boardman, David Fincher, Mary Ann Marino, Aris-
tides McGarry
Camera: Fredrick Elmes
Editing: Tim Squyres
Set Design: Jane Musky
Music: Mychael Danna
Cast: Clive Owen, Mason Lee, Sonom Gualson, Brian Smyj, Jamie Har-
ris, Jeff Jensen, Jarrod Bunch, Artie Malesci, Kevin Catucci, Losang
Gyatso, Satoru 'Sat' Tsufura
6 minutes

HULK (2003)
Director: **Ang Lee**
Screenplay: John Turman, Michael France, James Schamus
Producers: Avi Arad, Kevin Feige, Larry J. Franco, Gale Anne Hurd, Stan
Lee, James Schamus, Cheryl A. Tkach, David Womark
Camera: Fredrick Elmes
Editing: Tim Squyres
Set Design: Rick Heinrichs
Music: Danny Elfman
Cast: Eric Bana, Jennifer Connelly, Sam Elliot, Josh Lucas, Nick Nolte,
Paul Kersey, Cara Buono, Todd Tesen, Kevin Rankin, Celia Weston,
Mike Erwin, Lou Ferrigno, Stan Lee, Regi Davis, Craig Damon, Geof-
frey Scott, Regina McKee Redwing, Daniel Dae Kim, Daniella Kuhn,
Michel Kronenberg, David Kronenberg, Rhiannon Leigh Wryn, Lou
Richards, Jenn Gotzon, Louanne Kelley, Toni Kallen, Paul Hansen
Kim, John Littlefield, Lorenzo Caliender, Todd Lee Coralli, Johnny
Kasti, Eric Ware, Jesse Corti, Rob Swanson, Mark Atteberry, Eva
Burkley, Rondda Holeman, John Maraffi, Michael Papajohn, David
St. Pierre, Boni Yanagisawa, David Sutherland, Sean Mahon, Brett
Thatcher, Kirk B. B. Woller, Randy Neville, John Prosky, Amir Faray,
Ricardo Aguilar, Victor Rivers, Lyndon Karp
138 minutes

BROKEBACK MOUNTAIN (2005)
Director: **Ang Lee**
Screenplay: Larry McCurty, Diana Ossana
Producers: Scott Ferguson, Michael Hausman, Larry McCurty, Diana
    Ossana, Bill Pohlad, James Schamus, Tom Cox, Murray Ord
Camera: Rodrigo Prieto
Editing: Geraldine Peroni, Dylan Tichenor
Set Design: Judy Becker
Music: Gustavo Santaolalla
Cast: Heath Ledger, Jake Gyllenhaal, Randy Quaid, Valerie Planche,
    Dave Trimble, Victor Reyes, Lachlan Mackintosh, Michelle Wil-
    liams, Larry Reese, Marty Antonini, Tom Carey, Dan McDougall,
    Don Bland, Steven Cree Molison, Anne Hathaway, Duval Lang, Dean
    Barrett, Hannah Stewart, Scott Michael Campbell, Mary Liboiron,
    Graham Beckel, Kade Phillips, Steffen Cole Moser, Brooklynn Prouix,
    Keanna Dube, James Baker, Pete Seadon, Sarah Hyslop, Jacey Kenny,
    Jerry Callaghan, Cayla Wolever, Cheyenne Hill, Jake Church, Ken
    Zilka, John Tench, Linda Cardellini, Anna Faris, David Harbour, Kate
    Mara, Will Martin, Gary Lauder, Christian Fraser, Cam Sutherland,
    Roberta Maxwell, Peter McRobbie
134 minutes

ONE LAST RIDE (2005)
Director: Tony Vitale
Screenplay: Patrick Cupo
Producers: David E. Adams, Christian Arnold-Beutel, Craig Ayers,
    Patrick Cupo, John J. Kelly, Claire Kupchak, Solveig Langeland, **Ang
    Lee**, Bjorg Veland
Camera: Mark Doering-Powell
Editing: Gregory Hobson
Set Design: Debbie Andrews
Music: Josh G. Abrahams
Cast: Patrick Cupo, Robert Davi, Chazz Palminteri, Anita Barone, Jack
    Carter, Joe Marinelli, Mario Roccuzzo, Tracey Walter, Tony Lee, Lana
    Parrilla, Candice Azzara, Charles Durning, Josh Hutcherson, Annie
    Abbott, Ossie Beck, Claire Kupchak, Martin Morales, San San Tran,
    Ramon Sison, Sonya Eddy, Ira Katz
88 minutes

LUST, CAUTION (2007)
Director: **Ang Lee**
Screenplay: Eileen Chan, James Schamus, Hui-Ling Wang
Producers: Lloyd Chao, William Kong, James Schamus, **Ang Lee**, David
    Lee, Er-Dong Liu, Zhong-lun Ren, Darren Shaw, Dai Song, Doris Tse
Camera: Rodrigo Prieto
Editing: Tim Squyres
Set Design: Lai Pan
Music: Alexandre Desplat
Cast: Tony Chiu Wai Leung, Wei Tang, Joan Chen, Leehom Wang,
    Chung-Hua Tou, Chih-ying Chu, Yin-Hsuan Kao, Lawrence Ko,
    Johnson Yuen, Kar Lok Chin, Yan Su, Saifei He, Ruhul Song, Anupam
    Kher, Jie Liu, Hui-Ling Wang, Akiko Takeshita, Hayato Fujiki, Seto
    Masumi, Noriko Kohyama, Shayam Pathak, Gu Zhang-Ping, Gao Bo-
    Wen, Yu Qun, Yat-Tung Lau, Yu Lai Cheng, Yuji Kojima, Mizogomi
    Yoko, Minamikata Fumika, Anys Fatnassi, Tang Ya Jun, Shi Hong,
    Deng Wei, Li Dou
157 minutes

TAKING WOODSTOCK (2009)
Director: **Ang Lee**
Screenplay: James Schamus
Producers: Cella Costas, Patrick Cupo, Michael Hausman, **Ang Lee**, Da-
    vid Lee, David Sauers, James Schamus
Camera: Eric Gautier
Editing: Tim Squyres
Set Design: David Gropman
Music: Danny Elfman
Cast: Henry Goodman, Edward Hibbert, Imelda Staunton, Demetri
    Martin, Kevin Chamberlin, Lee Wong, Anthoula Katismatides, Clark
    Middleton, Bette Henritze, Sondra James, Jeffrey Dean Morgan,
    Christina Kirk, Gail Martino, Emile Hirsch, Adam LeFevre, Eugene
    Levy, Andy Prosky, Dan Fogler, Carmel Amit, Zachary Booth, Jen-
    nifer Merrill, Ivan Sandomire, Matthew Shear, Darcy Bledsoe, Halley
    Clanfarini, Jesse Kile, Ashley Middlebrook, Bec Stupak, Gabriel
    Sunday, Jonathan Groff, Mamie Gummer, Stephen Kunken, Adam
    Pally, Kevin Sussman, Pippa Pearthree, Skylar Astin, Daniel Eric
    Gold, Leonard Berdick, Sharon J. Giroux, William B. Ward Jr., Louisa

Krause, Spadaque Volcimus, Bill Coelius, Nick Taylor, Michael Izqui-
erdo, Katherine Waterston, Will Janowitz, Jeremy Shamos, Malachy
Cleary, Richard Thomas, Sebastian Beacon, Kelly Klein, Garett Ross,
Darren Pettie, Andrew Katz, Patrick Cupo, Boris McGiver, Liev
Schreiber, Caitlin FitzGerald, Michael J. Berg, Taunia Hottman-Hub-
bard, David Lavine, Michael Zegen, Andrew Zox, Angus Hamilton,
Christopher Meier, Richard Phelan McGreal, Casson Rugen, Joseph
Ulmer, Harry Zittel, Alyssa May Gold, Gaston Jean-Baptiste, Michael
McGinnis, Dan Knobler, Jon Seale, David Wilson Barnes, James Han-
lon, Stefano Da Fre, Don Puglisi, Kirsten Bach, Rachel Morrall, Paul
Dano, Kelli Garner, Marjorie Austrian, Kyle Plante, Lewis Zucker,
Heskethane Tallulah Bankhead

120 minutes

LIFE OF PI (2012)
Director: **Ang Lee**
Screenplay: David Magee
Producers: Kevin Richard Buxbaum, Jean-Christophe Castelli, William
    M. Connor, Dean Georgaris, **Ang Lee**, David Lee, Michael J. Malone,
    Gil Netter, Tabrez Noorani, Jesse Prupas, Pravesh Sahni, David
    Womark
Camera: Claudio Miranda
Editing: Tim Squyres
Set Design: David Gropman
Music: Mychael Danna
Cast: Suraj Sharma, Irrfan Khan, Ayush Tandon, Gautam Belur, Adil
    Hussain, Tabu, Ayaan Khan, Mohd. Abbas Khaleeli, Vibish Sivaku-
    mar, Rafe Spall, Gerard Depardieu, James Saito, Jun Naito, Andrea Di
    Stefano, Shravanthi Sainath, Elie Alouf, Padmini Ramachandran, T.
    M. Karthik, Amarendran Ramanan, Hari Mina Bala, Bo-Chieh Wang,
    I-Chen Ko, Jian-wei Huang, Ravi Natesan, Adyant Balaji, Chirag
    Agarwal, Ahan Andre Kamath, Om Kamath, Srilekh Katta, Swati Van
    Rijswijk, M. Keerthana, Indumohan Poornima, Josephine Nithya
    B., Samyuktha S., A. Deiva Sundari, G. Vasantakumary, A. Vithya,
    Mythill Prakash, Raj Patel, Hadiqa Hamid, Iswar Srikumar

127 minutes

Ang Lee: Interviews

The New Face of Taiwanese Cinema: An Interview with Ang Lee, Director of *The Wedding Banquet*

Chris Berry / 1993

From *Metro* magazine, no. 96 (Summer 1993–1994). Reprinted by permission.

New Taiwanese farce *The Wedding Banquet* is currently in release nation-wide, and distributors Palace Entertainment have high hopes for the film. Unlike the art films of Hou Hsiao-Hsien and Edward Yang like *Terrorizer*, *City of Sadness*, *The Puppetmaster*, and *A Brighter Summer's Day*, *The Wedding Banquet* is a popular mainstream film with crossover appeal to arthouse audiences. It has already won the Golden Bear at Berlin and had successful runs in Europe and the United States as well as Taiwan, where it was an enormous hit, doing US $4 million worth of business.

However, director Ang Lee was a worried man after the film opened the Melbourne International Film Festival earlier in the year. "In Seattle, it was a hundred times what happened yesterday. I got my first standing ovation. In San Francisco, it was even better," he fretted. I explained some cultural differences between Americans and Australians; Australians have a reputation for extroversion overseas, but back here they are more reserved. The crowd at the film festival might not have whooped and hollered, but they really did love the film.

This was ironic, because *The Wedding Banquet* explodes a few stereotypes about the Chinese, and also shows some of the cultural and generational differences amongst Chinese, just as the different reactions from Australians and Americans demonstrate that not all Anglo-Saxons are alike. *The Wedding Banquet* is about a Taiwanese gay man, Wai-Tung, who lives in New York with his lover, Simon. His parents back in Taipei do not know he is gay and keep pressuring him to get married. As the only son, it is his responsibility to produce grandsons and continue the family line. Meanwhile, his friend, mainland Chinese painter Wei-Wei, is in trouble because she needs a green card. Wai-Tung decides to kill two birds with one stone by marrying Wei-Wei. But when his elderly and infirm parents decide to attend the wedding, the farce really begins.

Whether in Taiwan, mainland China, Hong Kong, or elsewhere, Chinese society has a reputation for being very homophobic, so Lee was clearly taking a big risk with this topic. No one could have expected it to do as well as it has. "I think Taiwan is on the verge of accepting different values and so, all of a sudden, it's OK," he explains. "I'm pretty sure the male kissing scene is the first one in Taiwanese cinema. The audience were very quiet during that, but then it was alright. Traditional values are breaking apart in Taiwan and so people are trying to find different values and multiple values are becoming acceptable. This film came just in time to break the barrier."

The emergent multiculturalism of Taiwan may come as a surprise to most of us here in Australia, who think of Chinese culture as relatively homogenous. However, Taiwan is as much a diasporic culture as Australia, and both it and other Chinese communities outside mainland China are highly heterogeneous. "To me, I'm a mixture of many things and a confusion of many things," says Lee. "I'm not a native Taiwanese [his parents migrated from the mainland in 1949], so I'm an alien in a way in Taiwan today with the native Taiwanese push for independence. But when I go back to China, I'm Taiwanese. Then, I live in the States now. I'm sort of a foreigner everywhere. Of course, I identify with Chinese culture because that was my upbringing, but that becomes very abstract; it's the idea of China. And the sentiment of being Chinese is different in New York than it is in Taiwan or in China. Wherever you come from, whether it's China or Hong Kong or Taiwan, in New York, you're just Chinese; it's sort of generalized and merged, and people are drawn to each other by that abstract idea of being Chinese. In that way, it was natural to me to include all the different Chinese in New York City in the film, because that's a reflection of my life; a mixture of languages and characters. It's kind of natural to me."

Wai-Tung's homosexuality is a symbol of these internal cultural differences and the tensions and humor they generate within the Chinese community. Indeed, it is clear that although Lee himself is not gay, he identifies strongly with Wai-Tung. "The father in *The Wedding Banquet* is a Nationalist general. He believes tradition must go on; 'my family was demolished by the communists; the Gaos name must go on; this is my only son.' This is like myself, like my father. When I was born, he was so happy. He wanted to become a monk before he met my mother in Tai-wan because the whole family was liquidated by the communists. They were landlords and my father was a district administrator when he was very young. He was the only one to escape, and my mother was the only one who escaped from her family, too. When I was born, there was new hope for the Lee family, so I carried a lot of that burden. It's the same as Wai-Tung felt, except that I dramatized it by making him gay, meaning that he has to put a stop to that tradition, which is the ultimate chal-lenge to the patriarchal tradition."

However, at the same time, Lee makes it clear that he understands the father, too. This is one of the qualities that helps explain why a Tai-wanese movie has been successful where so many Hollywood comedies about homosexuality have failed. Unlike *Partners*, *La Cage Aux Foles* and so on, none of the humor in *The Wedding Banquet* is achieved at the ex-pense of any of the characters. The film takes a third person perspective that is common in all farces, because it gives us more knowledge than any one character has and so, for example, we can see the humor and ab-surdity of the fake marriage whereas they either cannot see it or cannot show that they see it. However, in addition, it draws on the old Chinese melodrama tradition of the forties and fifties to make this perspective a sympathetic one where we laugh out of understanding and not at the characters.

This melodramatic tradition, which would be well-known to Chinese filmgoers, gives the film a bitter-sweet quality which may not be im-mediately apparent to Western viewers. "For them, it's funny and emo-tional, and brings back some of the old family values," Lee says. "It's in-teresting for them to see a Chinese family go through such events. That's about it." For Chinese viewers, on the other hand, Lee believes the un-spoken pain and suffering that lies beneath the frothy surface punches home with more impact. "The happy ending is a myth. On the bottom it's very sad and sentimental, because everybody has to give up so much to get the happy ending. The wedding banquet ceremony is symbolic. To me, one of the better scenes is when the parents leave totally satisfied from the wedding banquet, and so I made the whole wedding banquet for that scene. The son looks at the parents leave, and it's so nice, and the bride feels like a real bride, and the old lawyer/driver shakes hands. I cried when I finished that scene. That was the last scene in the movie. We were wrapped when we finished that scene."

Another level to the film that Lee feels Western viewers may miss out on is that of political allegory. Because the groom comes from Taiwan and bride from mainland China, but the wedding, unbeknownst to the parents, is a fake one that takes place in New York, the situation is open to all sorts of interpretations. "I didn't do that deliberately, but it just happened that it worked out that way. Of course I was aware of it when I came up with the idea, and it fits perfectly. For example, I heard a lot of laughter during the speech the father gives about it being like the two Chinas coming back together. 'We should thank the ancestors because they have been watching over us'—that got a big laugh in Taipei. That worked much better there. People here laugh at the bit when the mother tries to stop the bride's tears, but they have no feeling whatsoever towards the father's speech. But, on the other hand, the audience in Taipei didn't find the marriage bureau scene so funny, because they aren't sensitive to the language of the New York municipal marriage bureau."

Although the film seems to have something for everyone and overall response has been favorable, some in Taiwan as well as the United States have criticized the yuppie lifestyle of the gay couple. "I have stretched about as far as I could," Lee argues. "If I went any further it wouldn't have been accepted. There was one gay film in Taiwan before. It was specifically about the gay community around the New Park, a very dark dingy community. There were no male kissing scenes and they stayed away from physical contact. It did very poorly and was considered a flop. But this is different because the relationship is like regular everyday life, and the film was set up that way so that straights would be open to the film. I'm pretty sure the male kissing scene is a first. It's taken for granted, which is different from the other movie."

Despite these criticisms, according to Lee, the box office success of *The Wedding Banquet* has created a demand amongst producers for more films that take up the old melodrama tradition in new ways and so attract big audiences. Over the last few years, the Taiwanese film industry has dwindled in the face of Hong Kong action pictures, to the extent that "If you want to make a movie, you cannot find a competent crew, because they all go to make commercials. You cannot find proper actors—they're singers or television actors."

Nevertheless, Lee is returning from many years living in the US to make his next film entirely in Taipei. Loosely translated as *Food, Drink, Men and Women*, "It's about a father who's a famous chef and his three unmarried daughters who all live together. It has multiple story lines and is a comedy about the struggle with desire." Let's hope it's as pleasant a surprise as *The Wedding Banquet*.

This article was first published in Metro *magazine, http://www.metromaga zine.com.au/index.html.*

Ang Lee Returned to His Native Taiwan to Make *Eat Drink Man Woman*

Steven Rea / 1994

From Knight Ridder/Tribune News Service, August 19, 1994. Reprinted by permission.

During the sumptuous four-minute opening-credits sequence of *Eat Drink Man Woman*, viewers get to see a deft display of culinary wizardry: the brisk chopping of exotic vegetables, the surgical preparation of sea bass, the bubbling pot of lotus flower soup. To shoot these scenes, Ang Lee, who co-wrote and directed this follow-up to his Oscar-nominated art-house hit *The Wedding Banquet*, employed a trio of top Taiwanese cooks. More than one hundred recipes were used in the film, which traces the relationship between three grown daughters and their widower father—a father who happens to be Taipei's most celebrated chef.

And that four-minute sequence? "It took eight shooting days," recalls Lee. "Long shooting days. From a production standpoint, the food was more difficult to work with than any actor. The challenge was how to bring the best out of the cuisine without looking like a food commercial. In order to capture the food as it was being prepared, and then as it was served, still steaming, we had to figure new ways to light it. We'd do it over and over again.

"Because, if it doesn't look exquisite, there's no point in doing it at all."

Eat Drink Man Woman is the final installment in what Lee jokingly calls his "Father Knows Best trilogy." A sweetly comic chronicle of familial and generational conflict (and of the major role food and sex play in our lives), it follows two other films in which Sihung Lung also starred as the family patriarch, "a symbol of Chinese tradition."

In Lee's first feature, 1991's *Pushing Hands*, the veteran Taiwanese actor played a tai-chi master growing increasingly despondent as he shared a house with his American daughter-in-law in a New York suburb. In *The Wedding Banquet*, Sihung was the retired general who comes to America only to discover that his son is involved in an intricate marital charade.

"It's kind of symbolic to see him facing the modern world, facing the family changes, seeing him confused and struggling," says Lee. "But it wasn't until the third film that I realized I was tailoring the role just for Sihung Lung, which is something I never did before. I've never written a role for a specific actor." And it wasn't until the third film that Lee, who has lived in the United States since 1978, when he enrolled in the theater program at the University of Illinois, returned to his homeland to shoot a movie from beginning to end. Unlike the crosscultural *Pushing Hands* and *Wedding Banquet*, *Eat Drink Man Woman* is set entirely in Taiwan.

"It is my homecoming movie," says Lee. "And there was a lot of pressure because this was a homecoming project and because there's a different working philosophy which takes ten times the director's energy."

"In Taiwan, it's much more of a director's show. Here, it's the producer who runs the production and the director pretty much just makes artistic decisions. . . . In Taiwan, you have to generate everything, initiate everything. People look to the director for everything. It was frankly cumbersome for me to do."

Following the commercial success and acclaim of last year's *The Wedding Banquet* (produced for $1 million, the film earned $30 million), scripts have been arriving at Lee's door with increasing frequency. "One involved a Chinese gangster, and a lot were 'heartwarming' family comedies," says Lee, adding that thus far nothing has piqued his interest. Instead, Lee will "lay back a little bit" before he delves into a new project. "I want to try to avoid being the flavor of the month."

Eat Drink Man Woman:
A Feast for the Eyes

Brooke Comer / 1995

From *American Cinematographer* 76, no. 1 (January 1995). Reprinted by permission.

"I'd always wanted to make a film about food," says director Ang Lee. "I wanted to make people salivate." Lee's previous project, *The Wedding Banquet*, featured fine dining, but did not sate his appetite for a full-blown food movie. *Wedding Banquet* did make Hollywood sit up and smell the wontons; the Academy Award nominee for Best Foreign Language Film cost only $1 million to make and grossed $23.6 million worldwide. The film's success allowed Lee to get more onscreen in *Eat Drink* despite a prix-fixe budget.

The story begins, and for the most part remains, in the Chu family kitchen. Tao Chu, Taiwan's greatest living chef, is in trouble. Food is his life, and he is losing his once-keen sense of taste. The three daughters he raised alone are now adults, still rebellious and still living at home. Culinary arts are in decline in Taiwan. Chu is depressed. He finds only temporary solace in his kitchen, preparing intricate gourmet dishes for his daughters.

Jia-Jen, the eldest, fears she'll be an old maid. Her passions are her work and her faith in Jesus Christ. Jia-Ning, the youngest, takes solace to extremes when she comforts her best friend's heartbroken boyfriend. Jia-Chien, an ambitious airline executive, is the only daughter who enjoys both cooking and an active sex life. "I started thinking about families and how they communicate," says the director. "Sometimes the things children need to hear most are the things parents find hardest to say, and vice versa. When that happens, we resort to ritual."

At this point in their lives, Chu family communications have been reduced to a Sunday night dinner. "Father Chu only knows how to satisfy

9

one of their basic needs—food," says Lee. "He prepares the most elaborate complex meals, yet his daughters are hardly able to eat the food, the one thing their father can give them." Throughout the film, food serves as a metaphor for love.

"Photographing food is very time-consuming," Lee points out. "My idea was to create shots that were so suggestive, people would salivate—and it wasn't easy. You can't just present beautiful food to tantalize an audience. You have to gear up the audience; you have to show it being prepared. You have to show the entire cooking process. In a film, you can't smell or taste the food. All you can do is see it. So how you see it becomes crucial. You're using food to seduce the senses."

Three world-class chefs worked on the production, including food consultant Lin Huei-Yi, daughter-in-law of China's leading food expert, Fu Pei-Mei. Huei-Yi coached the actors on physical preparation of dishes, and special choreography was devised to mimic traditional chefs' movements. Up to a dozen dishes had to be prepared, steaming and shiny, for an eight-second shot. "It would probably take two hours to film a peanut butter and jelly sandwich if the peanut butter had to be steaming," Lee muses. "Imagine filming Chi-Ling Fish, Steamed Deer in a Pumpkin Pot, or Lotus Flower Soup."

A scene in which Jia-Chien slices tofu to make dumplings for her boyfriend required six hours of shooting. For a scene in which she makes Chinese pancakes, there were two chefs making pancakes with three assistants. "A male chef would throw the dough on the griddle," recalls Lee, "but it wasn't possible for him to double his hand for Jia-Chien's, so a woman chef, a pancake expert, had to be on the set." In that scene, the pancakes are just a small part of a ten-course meal. Five backup dishes were prepared for every dish that was to appear on camera.

Lee's experience with food preparation precedes his career in film. Born in Taiwan, he came to America to study film. His primary exposure to cinema as a child was Hollywood movies and Taiwanese melodramas. "I was a movie freak when I was a child," he recalls. "I liked screwball comedy, I liked Billy Wilder, Italian neorealism, early Fellini, De Sica, and Bergman."

Lee earned an MFA from New York University and won Best Director and Best Film at the New York University Film Festival. He was packing to return to Taiwan when he got a call from an agent who'd seen his work and urged him to stay. "I spent six years writing scripts, pitching, and learning the basic screenplay structure, which they didn't teach me in school." While honing his filmmaking skills, Lee did all the cooking while his wife worked. "From a production standpoint," says the director, "food is the most difficult talent I've ever worked with."

Around the time Lee was looking for a producer for his film *Pushing Hands*, a new production company called Good Machine was looking for filmmakers with promising short films who had not yet made a feature. The co-principals, James Schamus and Ted Hope, liked Ang Lee's work and planned to contact the filmmaker about working with them. But he beat them to it, calling them first. Today, Good Machine is renowned as a leading production company in the independent scene. "No money was our strength at first," Schamus reflects. "We kept the company going by living off fees from co-productions and service deals. We made a conscious decision to avoid commercials and music videos. We chose our projects carefully."

The relationship between Good Machine and Lee remains solid. "With almost every filmmaker we work with," says Schamus, "we make a first feature with that person and stick with that person. The real reason is that in the low-budget world, the writer-director is the key figure in terms of marketing." He adds that cinematographers often stick closely with one director too. "Both parties often increase their skills in the course of their collaboration."

Schamus, neither a director nor a cinematographer, has increased his collaboration skills, having written both *Wedding Banquet* and *Eat Drink Man Woman* with Lee and Hui-Ling Wang. Lee calls Schamus "one of the best script doctors in the world." Lee also had experience in common with his cinematographer. Jong Lin shot the director's previous films *Wedding Banquet* and *Pushing Hands*, as well as projects for other directors including *Shadows of a Dream*, a finalist in the Tokyo Film Festival.

Lee smiles as he describes meeting Lin at NYU. "Jong didn't want to have anything to do with film. He wanted to do anything else in the world. He came from a film family that talked about film morning, noon, and night. He was fed up with film. He wanted no part of it."

Lin agrees. "I never thought, when I was studying at NYU, that I would end up being a cinematographer later on." Perhaps the shoes looked too big to fill. Lin's father was a top director of photography during the Chinese Golden era, the winner of four Golden Horse Awards (China's equivalent of the Academy Award), and is now the only cameraman in Taiwan to own a private film studio, Cine Kong, as well as a full-service rental house.

Lin's father also designed a mini Cinemascope zoom lens more than twenty years ago. "Back then," Lin explains, "some major brand zooms were too expensive, so my father made his own." For special effects films, Lin Sr. designed a home-made optical printer with a Mitchell movement.

From the age of thirteen, the younger Lin spent summers carrying batteries on his father's films. After studying French literature at Tamkang University in Taiwan, and doing a hitch in the army, Lin went to NYU film school. "Even then, I didn't think cinematography would be a career, until I got so many offers from classmates to shoot their films." He admits that his strong technical background and early training were a boon. "I'm very fortunate," says Lin, "to have had steady work ever since."

"Jong has a strong sense of cinematography," Lee explains, "but he won't let light or a look take over a film. You'll never watch one of his films and say 'Wow, great cinematography,' and forget the story. He knows how to bring out characters." Lee usually goes over a script scene by scene with Lin, and tells him what kinds of mood and emotion he's after. "Then he's on his own. And most of the time, I agree with his decisions."

The two developed a shorthand means of communication sprinkled with film history references. "Occasionally if we'd take the camera up and intercut an angle, I'd say to Jong, 'Aha! A Bergman confession angle!' Or in the scene when the youngest Chu daughter is at work in a fast food restaurant, feeling guilty about taking away her best friend's boyfriend, we used toplight to get a certain shadow. We called it 'the Bergman guilty light.' We made up our own terms as we went along."

Lee's talent for storytelling keeps his emphasis entrenched in the characters, in propelling the story along, rather than making pretty pictures. "In many movies, from Hong Kong to Hollywood, there is a tendency for so-called good cinematography to take over the story. But I always focus on the story, and sometimes I'm not very fair to Jong," says Lee. "His camera work is invisible. I want people to forget about cinematography. Of course, I want good quality cinematography. But working with me, Jong has less of a chance to win a Golden Horse award for best cinematography."

The filmmaking team was unable to screen dailies during the shoot, and by the time production was completed, they'd only seen one third of the rushes. "Jong and I discussed it," says Lee. "We chose to send the film to DuArt, because it's such a good lab and we couldn't get that kind of quality in Taipei." The cost of having the developed film sent back was prohibitive. Instead, selected work prints were transferred to tape and sent back to Taiwan on cassette. Lee and Lin's dailies were limited to the material on the tapes, which arrived long after the scenes had been completed.

"We had to do a lot of guessing during production," Lee admits. "And it was hard, especially with the complications of the food. You really can't be sure until you see the rushes." Lee saved the food scenes for the last, "so I had absolutely no idea how they'd come out. I didn't see them until two months after we'd wrapped. Luckily, they looked fine." But he admits that if he'd had more of a budget, "I'd have had the rushes sent over."

For the food scenes in the Chu kitchen in the opening of the film, Lin used a heavy grid cloth to build a soft light box. "I used 5K HMIs through the grid cloth, and sometimes mixed in harsher light too, in case the color of the food tended to be darker," he explains. For scenes in the dining room, he also used the technique over the dining room table, this time using a Lowel light behind the grid.

A Panther dolly with a jib arm allowed Lin to move the camera through the kitchen during the whole shoot. "We tried to make it look like a star-tour," he explains. "I operated the Steadicam with an Arri III camera and a 9.8mm super-wide-angle lens. To create the chaos scenes—like the one in the kitchen of the Grand Hotel and the fight scene at the Chu house— I used a handheld camera and covered with master shots from different angles. The handheld shots could be improvised, as long as they didn't cross the line, because they could be cut together very well."

The most elegant location in the picture is undoubtedly the Grand Hotel, renowned as one of the most luxurious properties in the world, and featuring what is reputedly the biggest kitchen in Taiwan. The wedding banquet scene featured in the film was not contrived; Lee managed to film preparations for an actual banquet. "The production was lucky to have permission to shoot a wide shot as a transition shot, to get the chaos scene in that kitchen," Lin observes. "At night, the camera crew was asked to be very efficient and finish shooting in two hours." In order to meet this strict requirement, Lin used minimum lighting, and an Arri III. "The banquet was a normal one for a wealthy Taiwanese family," Lin explains. "There must have been 120 tables, each one with twelve guests." He adds that the filmmakers were lucky enough to get some cameo shots, including closeups of Taiwan's minister of internal affairs. "When the film opens in Taiwan," Lin observes, "the audience will crack up when they see him."

Real locations lent authenticity to *Eat Drink*. Most of the crucial scenes took place in the Chu family home, in particular the kitchen. Lee chose the ex-mayor's house, a stately fifty-year-old mansion built in the Japanese tradition. The fact that it was abandoned was a plus; it meant some cleaning up, but it also meant Lee could have the interior rebuilt. "I wanted a living room without walls for mise-en-scene, for an open feeling and so you could see people better." He had glass doors separate the big kitchen for depth, and he let the windows remain. "The big Japanese windows give good shadow depth to the images," according to Lee.

Two school scenes were mounted at real schools. The eldest Chu daughter is a high school teacher, and several scenes track her blossoming romance with a volleyball instructor. The school Lee chose was "very supportive," he remembers. "We were there for a week, and everyone was very excited to have a film crew around. We used students as extras." In another scene, Father Chu begins to prepare lunch for Shan-Shan, a neighbor's little girl, to take to school. Suddenly Shan-Shan's lunchbox is the envy of her classmates, and she begins to take requests from them, which she passes on to the chef. Lee used the actual school that Yu-Chien Tang, the child playing Shan-Shan, attends, and her real classmates played themselves. "We couldn't have done that in New York," Lee notes.

Shooting in Taiwan, according to the director, is different from shooting in America from bureaucratic as well as technical points of view. "There is a different work ethic in Taiwan," he notes. "In the States, a producer runs a production. The director asks what the producer wants. That's how artistic choices are made. In Taiwan, the director has more clout. Organization is less efficient, but there is more loyalty. You're not pushed as much in terms of time."

The role of the cinematographer is different in Taiwan as well. "The head gaffer deals with a lot of the lighting," Lee explains. "You tell the gaffer what kind of mood you want and he executes it. He stands next to the camera and works with the assistant. In Taiwan, gaffers have a lot of experience. It's not surprising to find a head gaffer who's been doing it for forty years. You also find more experienced camera crews."

Production sound mixer Tom Paul had his own frustrations; in order to set up the microphones properly, he needed a lot of C-stands and flags to get rid of the boom shadows. But the crew could only use tape and black cardboard stuck on the ceiling or walls to eliminate shadow. While shooting a kitchen scene in which Jia-Chien cooks for her boyfriend, for example, Lee wanted the actress to walk back and forth, despite the small space of the kitchen. "This was tough for Tom," observes Lin. "It required a lot of boom work, so gaffer Chin-Fou spent a lot of time rigging pieces of black cardboard on the ceiling to help Tom's boom. Then we started to roll the camera and film. But during the middle of the take, the cardboard pieces fell from the ceiling one by one. We all burst out laughing."

There were tense moments when a steaming dish had to be captured on film before it lost its perfect gloss, but Lee notes that generally speaking, "nothing went really wrong. In fact, the food shots came out especially well despite the conditions and our not being able to screen dailies."

Lee knew his film was a success when he made Michael Tong smack his lips. Tong, owner of New York's Shun Lee restaurant, added to his menu several entrees from the film (which includes cuisines from Shanghai, Hunan, Peking, and Beijing). Film fans can order Dragon Swimming on Yellow Sea (lobster and sliced kiwi, preparation time: six hours), or Beggar's Chicken (chicken cooked in clay), or Jade Shrimps Swimming in Jelly Lake (shrimp and steamed egg). "It's hard," says Tong, whose entrees have been photographed for numerous magazines, "to make food look good on camera. It has to be piping hot, under a sheen of glaze. After ten minutes, that shine disappears and the food is visually uninteresting." He applauds Lee's efforts. "This film will make people hungry," he predicts.

One small problem arose when customs officials refused to let a cassette containing dailies material leave America, fearing the film was catering to a more prurient kind of appetite. "They thought it was a porno film because of the title," says Lee. "I was really mad then because they held the tape for a week. But now I laugh when I think about it."

Schtick and Seduction

Graham Fuller / 1996

From *Sight and Sound* 6, no. 3 (March 1996): 24. Reprinted by permission.

Sense and Sensibility's hired-gun director Ang Lee could expect many baptisms of fire working on his first Hollywood-financed film. Not the least of them was the prospect of directing a cast of British actors that included Emma Thompson, who'd written the screenplay; the newly consecrated Hugh Grant; thesp of thesps Alan Rickman; and wet-behind-the-ears newcomers Kate Winslet and Greg Wise. Lee was no stranger to formidable actors, having directed the Chinese actor Sihung Lung in previous movies. But in the Taiwanese film industry the director is God and brooks no arguments from stars. By all accounts (including his own, which follows) he didn't take an iron-fist-in-a-velvet-glove approach, but there was no doubt who was boss.

Graham Fuller: This was your first serious experience of working with Western actors. What was your initial impression of how it was going to proceed once shooting started?

Ang Lee: On the first couple of days on *Sense and Sensibility*, I really had a problem, especially with the stars, who had the attitude that they were going to carry the movie. This is really the opposite to Taiwan, where you make movies that will carry the actors. But after a while, we started not so much to negotiate, but to appreciate what each other was doing and find a common ground that was best for the movie. I found my role was to seduce the best out of everybody and try to fit all their different styles into one movie. Technically, my main job was to bring the performances down.

GF: How did you go about that?

AL: When I'm shooting, what I do is very physical and technical. I don't go through a lot of thoughts. I knew I was working with brilliant actors and actresses, so we spent the rehearsal time not rehearsing but talking about the relationships—for days and days. Once we'd blocked a scene, it was in their hands. But I wouldn't let them think too much; they weren't allowed to watch rushes and get self-conscious.

GF: How did you work with Kate Winslet (Marianne Dashwood)? She had limited film experience.

AL: Kate was not an accomplished actress. I had seen her in *Heavenly Creatures* [1994]. I said to myself, "There is a possible Marianne. She could be tragic or horrific in the part if I don't bring grace out of her; could be torture having her say those lines from Jane Austen." When I cast her she'd just turned nineteen. She's a bold, raw talent, and can do anything, but is very difficult to control. She's probably the actor I spent most time with, other than Emma, as the writer and in the casting process, too.

We were putting Kate against Emma in many scenes. This was one of the greatest difficulties I faced. Emma is brilliant, and she could make Kate seem not so good. And, in a film about sense and sensibility, I was very nervous about that. Young actresses don't know how to concentrate, and by trying too hard, they weaken their acting abilities and risk looking ridiculous. So I did a lot of internal breathing and voice exercises with Kate, and some Chi relaxing exercises to help her reduce tension and let go of little habits. I am not an expert on English speech, so Kate and Emma discussed that together; they also spent time being like sisters.

Then we gave Kate Gothic novels to read. There was a danger that they would make her go over the top, but we wanted to use the best of that. The secret for me was to make it funny, although Kate had to be sincere at all times, even in this silly Gothic atmosphere. Other than how to light Kate, it took me at least a couple of weeks shooting and watching dailies to find the secret of how to get Marianne on the screen. Kate had a tendency to frown, to smile too broadly, and to tuck her chin in. It was useful to her to be told by me that she did these physical things; I think she'll remember it for the rest of her life.

Direction has to be very simple, or you'll confuse the actors. I gave Kate her directions shortly before I rolled the camera and after we'd agreed on what to do. We'd do one take, then another very quickly: I didn't give her too much time. The other actors were too sophisticated; it would be absurd to work with them this way. When I did occasionally, they'd feel a little uncomfortable. But Kate was different; she was willing to try anything.

GF: Given that Emma Thompson had been writing the script for five years and presumably knew her character, Elinor Dashwood, better than anyone, how did you approach getting what you wanted from her?

AL: Emma's two roles contradicted each other: usually you don't allow the writer on the set because they get upset. Dealing with her was two different jobs. It's good I had almost six months of pre-production while she was rewriting, otherwise I'd have felt I was snatching the baby from her hands. She and Lindsay [Doran] were the mothers of the project; I felt I was the stepfather. I was fresh to it, as the director, and as a foreigner to the material. I got into it through the rewrites and the production design, and involved Emma in my concept for the movie. In terms of dealing with her as the writer, I figured I had to put her ego aside if we wanted to make the film work. I think she appreciated what I wanted to do, and I learned a lot from her performance and her interpretation of the text.

Emma was way too old to play Elinor. The biggest job was to reduce her age. I did everything I could to relax her—gave her exercises, like Kate. She also worked on her voice; she was not allowed to go below a certain register. Emma is very open minded to physical acting; she likes full body shots, shots from the back, long shots. To create the Elinor image, I would tell her what kind of frame I was putting her in; it's the first time I'd worked with an actress that way. I'd shoot Emma gradually turning from her back, to profile, to close shot; Kate's was the opposite, from front shot, to profile, to back. This was to show the transformations in their characters. Elinor gets more romantic; Marianne becomes more reasonable. They gradually change position through the course of the film. The climax is the Cleveland sequence, the most cinematic in the movie. Marianne goes up the hill and Brandon brings her back to the sick bed. I built a set for that sick bed and filmed it with a top shot; it's the *Sense and Sensibility* shot. Desperate Elinor discovers that Marianne's her soulmate; and if Marianne dies, she'll die, too. I told Emma to show pure fear and remove every other emotion. She did extremely well.

GF: Alan Rickman has a swashbuckling quality, which is exactly what his character, Colonel Brandon, lacks. How did you get such a perfectly low-key performance from him?

AL: I respect Alan as an actor in the English style—the big speech style. He could read from a telephone book and it would sound interesting. But this wouldn't do for Brandon, who, in the book, is boring, and a loser in the romantic story. You sense Marianne settles for less because she doesn't get Willoughby; that's not exactly what you want a film audience to think. Emma said Brandon was the most difficult role to adapt, but I think she gave him manhood and made him a really solid person, who not only takes care of himself but takes care of others. Instead of playing up his unattractiveness and his age, she played up his tragic history, which is really acceptable to the audience in making him a lover for Marianne. Still, it was necessary for Alan to "reduce." When he did, I asked him to do "more." Naturally, he got confused; I meant he should reduce more.

GF: Did he want to be more flamboyant?

AL: He wanted to be romantic. He saw Brandon as more romantic than he is in the book. But I think that romantic side should all be in the head and shouldn't show. Anytime it did show, we cut it down. But Alan was the one actor I just set loose after our initial communication. I was quite enchanted with his performance; the others required more struggle.

GF: You cast Greg Wise as Willoughby, the seducer, who is flamboyant. But did you have to "reduce" him, too?

AL: Yes. In casting Willoughby, I wanted somebody who could play an athletic Byron, but not dangerous in that James Dean way. Greg came in and gave an astonishing reading, and he showed he really wanted the job by bringing flowers, like Willoughby does in the book. He was not a name, but we were all very struck by him. He's the most delightful person, a good sportsman; he knew how to handle Willoughby's coracle, which was very dangerous. The problem with him was that he's not really *up there* yet, and among all this acting caliber, he really had to be the most charming person in the movie. It's easy for a young actor to be insecure, and overact. The performance can become snotty and then it becomes unintentionally funny. I'd constantly say to Greg, "You're very attractive; don't try to show us anything. The others will carry the plot." I'd have to keep telling him he was great. At other times, I was very cruel with him, like I've been to young Chinese actors. Not everything he did was right, and I'd say, "Don't do this, don't do that." Like Kate, he'd take it in, because he's young.

GF: As Edward Ferrars, you had Hugh Grant, almost a superstar. How did you work with him?

AL: The first couple of days I had a problem with him, because he had that star shtick to do. He wanted to do things I didn't think fitted. Finally, we came to a common ground. I figured I had to let him do what he does best to save the character. Edward is sheepish and wimpy in the book, but in the movie we needed somebody who could come in for fifteen minutes, leave for eighty pages, come back, steal the last scene, and break your heart. You need a really fine actor to do that.

Edward's saving grace is his dry sense of humor: he uses it to rebel against society, almost in a heroic way. I can't think of anybody since Cary Grant who can do that as well as Hugh. So it was necessary for me to take a step back and let him go with that. Meanwhile, he had to take a step back and reduce it in the more serious moments. He was very co-operative.

GF: Did he want to bumble and stutter more?

AL: Yes. Sometimes I could not cope with his elaborate vocal skills, so I did imitations of him. It deeply hurt him, but we got used to each other. Probably the most direct language I used, I used with him. I was blunt, the only way I knew how to convey honestly what I wanted. With the other actors, I'd have twelve nicer ways of putting it. It became a very satisfactory working relationship with Hugh, probably the most pleasing of all.

The Angle on Ang Lee

Oren Moverman / 1997

Originally published in *Interview* magazine, September 1997. Courtesy BMP Media Holdings, LLC.

Some directors dazzle us with films that are slick, cool, and stylish. Ang Lee's are none of those things especially, but reveal instead the wisdom of a truly great storyteller.

Ang Lee reigns supreme in the void that periodically opens up between Hollywood corporate filmmaking and the independent movement's flavor-of-the-month feeding frenzy. A quiet, gentle but commanding presence, this Taiwanese-born, New York University–educated director has connected with audiences throughout the world by concentrating on a component that is equally neglected on both ends of the cinematic spectrum: the human being. With *Pushing Hands* (1992), *The Wedding Banquet* (1993), *Eat Drink Man Woman* (1994), and *Sense and Sensibility* (1995), Lee moved effortlessly through three continents and two centuries, evolving as a perceptive, always entertaining cultural observer. In doing so, he was attacked for lacking an auteur's vision; critics could not pigeonhole him as an aesthete, and he became known as an "actor's director," a term usually used as a consolation prize for a popular filmmaker who has failed to impress the eye with an inimitable visual style. Yet Lee's humanism transcends such qualms.

His powerful new film, *The Ice Storm*, shows him once again crossing cultural boundaries. Based on the 1994 novel by Rick Moody, it's a Watergate-era period piece about two affluent, frigid families in New Canaan, Connecticut, who get caught up in that time's aimless winds of change and spiral into emotional and spiritual numbness. Set against the backdrop of a freakish weather calamity, the film is a stylized day-in-the-life look at the events that lead to the story's tragic, strangely cathartic end. The excellent ensemble includes Kevin Kline, Sigourney Weaver,

Joan Allen, Christina Ricci, Elijah Wood, Tobey Maguire, and Adam Hann-Byrd, but *The Ice Storm*'s real star is its unpretentious helmer, who still believes in his audience's ability to feel.

Oren Moverman: After *Sense and Sensibility*, you became known as a director who refuses to tie his vision to a particular landscape or time period. Your main interest is *people*. What appealed to you about the American suburban seventies characters of *The Ice Storm*?

Ang Lee: Nothing personal, I assure you. Living in Taipei in the seventies, I knew some things about American suburban life and the sexual revolution of the late sixties from reading about them. But it was all somewhat vague to me. James [Schamus, co-producer and screenwriter of *The Ice Storm*] gave me the book to read, and 210 pages into it, I saw a possible movie. It was the scene where the father, Ben Hood [played in the film by Kevin Kline], finds his neighbor's son's body. Something about that hit me really hard; it was almost like a Greek tragedy. I kept asking myself, Why did the kid have to die? It wasn't justified retribution.

OM: It's interesting that you saw an element of Greek tragedy, because both the book and James Schamus's adaptation are funny in a very modern way.

AL: Yes, it's a story about embarrassment and a kid's anguish. I'm a filmmaker who does family dramas. You can say all kinds of negative things about the family and its many different forms. But when Paul, the film's narrator and oldest kid, sees his family collapsing after the ice storm, it's very emotional, very moving. So I got sucked into the project. There was a certain innocence about that time; the parents were even more adolescent than the kids. And then there's this visual metaphor—the ice storm—that changes their lives. It's not about a natural disaster, but a human-nature disaster tied to a specific time and place. But at heart, the basic human desires and needs are the same from race to race, culture to culture, time to time. That's why someone like me is allowed to make these movies.

OM: This is your first American film dealing strictly with American culture. But your love affair with America started in 1978, didn't it?

AL: I came here to study film. Well, that's what most people in Taiwan did back then—went to the States for higher education. If you got a Ph.D. or a master's degree at a well-known American college, when you came back—you know, you could have a better life. [*laughs*] I never imagined a Chinese filmmaker could make a movie here, but then an agent convinced me to stay. He was very persuasive. *The Ice Storm* is an American movie, but it's not the way I imagined this country when I watched American films in my childhood.

OM: It's closer to reality because it's about antiheroes, as opposed to Hollywood heroes. The characters in the film are really bored and lost and confused by false liberation. What do you think is missing from their lives that allows nature to come in and wreak such havoc?

AL: I wish I knew the answer. These characters have so many reasons why they're unhappy, or why they distrust each other, or why their needs are not fulfilled. It's very hard to point out exactly what the cause is. I think it's many reasons from the past, and many unknowns of the future. The characters have pop psychology, fashion, polyester, the idea of an open marriage, liberation, desire, fulfillment—but where do they go? I don't know. How confusing! I cannot say why the characters behave the way they do. But that, to me, is the essence of life.

OM: Do you think that as an outsider it's easier for you to understand the tension between nature and the story's spiritually frozen people—easier, say, than if you were an American?

AL: It's probably initially clearer to me than to people who grew up here and relate to the material in a personal way. Of course my weakness was understanding the texture. I had to catch up. But the film's perspective on nature is, I think, Oriental. For me nature is an active force, something you have to fear and respect. That's related to how I grew up. It's probably different from an American perspective. But honestly, I can't tell any more which part of me is American and which is Oriental. I've lived here a long time, and my upbringing in Taiwan had a lot of American influences. Of course as an outsider directing English-language movies, I have to make more guesses, because I know less. But those guesses could also be more accurate, more objective, because I have to do a lot more observation and show a lot of sympathy to the characters—and sympathizing is good when you direct a movie.

OM: Why do you use the family structure as the basis for all of your films?

AL: Family life to me is very solid. It provides beliefs that can keep you from boredom, from being destructive. These usually involve bondage of some sort—social bondage, family, nation, religion. But it gets very complex.

OM: You constantly examine the role of the father figure in your work. In fact you jokingly referred to your first three films as the "Father Knows Best" trilogy. In *Sense and Sensibility*, it's the absence of a father figure that sets everything in motion. In *The Ice Storm*, we see TV images of the ultimate American father figure, the president, Richard Nixon, at the time of his fall from grace, and everything is thrown into chaos. Ben, the Kevin Kline character, is the more immediate father figure in crisis. Why do you use the theme of the father so much? Is it something personal?

AL: Because Chinese society is a patriarchal society, I have always thought the father figure has bigger meaning than just the parent—it's the symbol of how tradition works. And in my first three movies, I used my father as a model.

OM: Tell me about him.

AL: My father's entire family was executed in China, but he escaped—he was the only one. He came to Taiwan, where he married my mother and they had me. He was the principal at my high school, which was one of the best high schools in Taiwan. It was always embarrassing to be the principal's son! And I was the first son, so I always felt everything rested on my shoulders. There was no love of art or creativity, not to mention the entertainment business, in our family. The whole father thing, family duty—it made it hard to breathe, hard to face your true self.

OM: What did your father want you to be?

AL: Anything but a filmmaker, I guess. He wanted me to teach, but I insisted on going to film school. If I hadn't ended up making *The Wedding Banquet* and winning awards for it, I would have been a disgrace to him.

   In *The Ice Storm* it was important to me to take on the father issue, because Ben is more evolved than the fathers in my other films. We used the father figure as the anchor, and cast the movie around him. But this time I used myself as the model.

OM: Yourself?

AL: Myself. My fear of being a father.

OM: In what way?

AL: I have two kids, thirteen and seven years old, and how I see myself as a parent is different from how I see my own father. It's not so much adults who produce children nowadays—it's really children who produce adults. You have to behave in such a way that your children look up to you, but you have to match it with effort, and you have to be a nice guy. Children push you to be more mature, but you're never prepared to be a role model and teach kids what to do and give them what they want. You always fear you're not good enough, so you just pretend. It's like directing a movie: You have some idea, but a lot of acting is going on in both roles. [*laughs*] You want to be honest with your kids, but you cannot totally. It would be like the movie *Liar Liar*—chaos. But as a parent, you have to keep things in order. Not like the parents in *The Ice Storm*, who are rushing bullheaded toward the unknown.

OM: You seem to understand the characters in your films, or at least what their problems are. But what I think is most extraordinary in your approach is that you don't judge them.

AL: There's a reason why people do things, and it isn't a director's job to judge them; that's up to the audience. Actors should provoke thoughts and emotions—that's what movies are about, not telling audiences how to feel.

OM: It seems as though you always manage to make your actors feel relaxed, unself-conscious, and yet focused. We've come to expect that from your films. What's different about *The Ice Storm* is that it has a very conscious style. We can see your fingerprints on it, whereas in the past you've said that you don't want people to see them.

AL: Yes, it has my fingerprints on it. I think this sort of intense material needs a style, otherwise it won't hold up. Because nature, in its naked structure, is so patchy, you have to make visual parallels and pull the film together carefully. It's not like you're watching just a story, as in *Sense and Sensibility*. In this film you're watching a progression of moments, so it's more artificial—or artsy, if you will—than the others I've made. It's great fun to work like that, but it's also painful, because it's a little unnatural to me. But it's a good stretch, I believe.

OM: One of the philosophical questions raised by *The Ice Storm* is echoed in Atom Egoyan's upcoming *The Sweet Hereafter*. Both of you seem to be asking: What are we doing to our children?

AL: I think it's part of the collective consciousness. The Chinese believe that if you do something wrong and nothing happens to you, it just means it's not time yet. Being parents, of course, we are sensitive to the question of what we are doing to our children. We're bouncing back to being cautious about the environment and our own behavior. We think of the consequences. We've got to be careful about what we do for our own convenience, about our own liberation, because all of that affects our children. Asking the right questions forces us to be better people, I hope. Movies and my family are the most important things to me. I try to keep them balanced, but my family has made sacrifices for my work. Because movies involve people who have put their dreams on my shoulders, it's something larger than my own life. It's a tough balancing act, like that trick where you try to keep plates whirling on poles without dropping them. It's very Chinese!

OM: There's a moment in *The Ice Storm* where one of the fathers comes up the stairs with a suitcase. He stops by his sons' room and says, "Hi, I'm back." The two boys look up baffled and ask, "Were you gone?"
AL: [*laughs*] It's very sad. The characters are sleepwalking through their lives. And then there's a wake-up call.

OM: But can't they have the wake-up call without the tragedy?
AL: No. Pain is the best wake-up call. I think pain can be a good thing, spiritually—a symptom that makes you realize what's going on. If you take the pain nerves out of your system, you are unprotected, you don't know when things go wrong. Real pain makes you grow.

OM: How have you grown as a filmmaker?
AL: I started out with three personal films. But what you know about, your neighborhood, can be very limiting, I think. That's why I wouldn't make ten films like that. Because my life growing up was pretty boring, I want to play, I want to stretch, explore. Every time I make a new film now, I think it's going to be a flop, that my number is up, and I like that. I don't want to fall, but I do want to see where the edge is—that's my attitude toward film. But I don't want to be a slave to moviemaking. I'll do what I have to do to make it work, but once a film is done, it's time to move one notch higher. To me, directing is about learning, *life* is about learning. Learning is not a way of getting your goal—it's the goal itself. It's the texture to life.

The Morning After

Godfrey Cheshire / 1997

From *Filmmaker* 6, no. 1 (September 1997): 42–43, 89. Reprinted by permission.

Much as its title signals an unpredictable change of weather, *The Ice Storm* marks an abrupt shift in the creative environment shared by Ang Lee and James Schamus. Nor is it the first. After the two collaborated on *Pushing Hands*, *The Wedding Banquet*, and *Eat Drink Man Woman*—with Lee as writer-director and Schamus as writer-producer—it seemed they had settled into a comfortable groove of making modestly scaled, enormously successful comedies about the emotional permutations of modern Taiwanese families. Then came 1995's *Sense and Sensibility*, a flying leap over to Jane Austen's England that also ushered Lee and Schamus into the realm of big-budget, star-powered moviemaking and serious Hollywood recognition: the film garnered seven Oscar nominations, winning one for Emma Thompson's screenplay.

The Ice Storm returns the team to their New York base (where Schamus also teaches film at Columbia University and helps direct the multifarious activities of Good Machine, the production company he runs with Ted Hope). Yet as much as it's a homecoming, the new film is also another departure. Adapted from Rick Moody's well-regarded 1994 novel, it's the first of Lee's films entirely scripted by Schamus. With a cast led by Sigourney Weaver, Kevin Kline, Joan Allen, and Christina Ricci, it's the team's first encounter with big-name American actors. And as a depiction of the unfettered sexual mores and corroding social conventions of the Nixon era, the film ventures a novel depiction of a familiar, yet oddly uncomfortable, zeitgeist: It's a backflip into a world of tacky clothes and even tackier behavior.

Set in suburban Connecticut in November 1973, as a blast of arctic weather prepares to throttle the Northeast, the story makes acerbic fun of the Sexual Revolution's retrospective embarrassments; its adults make a nervous game of infidelity while their kids pursue erotic initiation as if its playfulness were a solemn duty. Nominally all this is phrased as comedy, yet the film aims for something far more complex and risky than the usual genre guidelines allow: Lee's extraordinarily nuanced direction and Schamus's probing delineations of character (his work captured the Best Screenplay prize at Cannes) combine to suggest the inevitably bitter flavor that comes with serious self-scrutiny, whether personal or collective. That sort of scrupulous thoughtfulness, however, remains a distinguishing characteristic of both Lee and Schamus—not only onscreen but even as they ponder their latest collaboration.

Filmmaker: Ang, what made you decide to make this film? You said you had some reservations about it.
Lee: *The Ice Storm* is harsher in many ways [than my other films]. Darker. I've never tried that before. It might just be everyday life to some other director, but to me, I make movies that are very comfortable to watch. This film is a challenge.

Filmmaker: It has a very tricky mix of tones.
Schamus: We always say, what's the risk, what's the gain? How do we take [the audience] to a comedic brink, get them off guard, and push them into the tragedy without pissing them off. That's high-risk filmmaking. We were walking in the border space between genres.

Filmmaker: Ang, did you read the novel or James's screenplay first?
Lee: I read the novel, and it really moved me. Especially toward the end when the train arrives and Paul Hood sees his family standing there. Another thing—I got to do an ice storm. It's my obsession. It's a very powerful metaphor, a parallel of what was going on with the family structure that particular year—lost innocence. Watergate. It was the year of "funny-looking," "tacky."

Filmmaker: Was it essential that the film be set in 1973? Did you consider setting it today?
Lee: I think the [film's] conflict is universal and immortal. But I think it's more sharp and heavy this way. You have no choice. [The period] sucks you in. It's a place that provides you emotional warmth and security and, at the same time, you try to liberate yourself from it and flee. Binding and liberating forces come back and forth. And [setting the film at] a changing time gives a feeling about this sort of Oriental philosophy—nothing

stands still. You have to constantly change. There's nothing you can rely on because things will change.

Schamus: *The Ice Storm* is probably the most "period" period film I've been involved with. For me, the major dismay is, oh my God, I grew up in a period! I'm old! But, yeah, the fractured orbits in which these family members are moving are of that time.

Filmmaker: The overthrow of Nixon—that was something really unusual in American politics. The President is our father and you're not supposed to hurt our father.

Schamus: That's absolutely right. [Watergate] did open the gates to a kind of Oedipal rage. But when we look at that period now, it triggers a different kind of rage having to do with the clothes!

Filmmaker: What's really frightening is that all this stuff is coming back in fashion again.

Schamus: Sigourney said it best—if you wore it the first time, you really shouldn't wear it the second.

Filmmaker: What were the main things that determined your visual approach to this? What did you go into thinking about in terms of the visual style?

Lee: Tacky was the essence. Something tacky is interesting. Something that worked against nature. Something man-made. And in terms of shooting, photorealism. Where people's eyes are, the focus—they're not looking at each other. Dreamy, unfocused, very intense—that was the objective. Also, working with the snow. The way I treated the ice storm, with fast, deep reflections. It made it very transparent and liberating. [One] looks through reflective surfaces, but at the same time feels naked.

Filmmaker: Someone said something interesting to me after the film, which was they thought you recreated the period more through emotions than through the outward ways people usually recreate the period.

Lee: I think that's more important. The emotion was why I wanted to make it.

Filmmaker: There's a great deal of anger in the film's depiction of family relations.

Schamus: The film carries with it a certain clarity that is adolescent or pre-adolescent in terms of its reality—ideas of justice, retribution, morality, what's fair. I hope the film says that we're not endorsing [that adolescent view] but that we understand those feelings. There is an acceptance of anger without the film being a product of that anger. Not that that anger should be coopted or muted, but it should exist alongside other feelings and ideas. And that's a more adult point of view.

Filmmaker: Did you work with the actors much in terms of what that period was like? Your older actors would have had their own memories of that period.

Lee: On the contrary. The crew was about our age and I knew most of how to make this movie by interviewing people on the crew. I thought I was making a documentary; I listened to them talk about their teens. [The younger siblings in the film would now be] about my age or a little younger. I grew up with these kids so I identify [with them]. And now they're their parents' age. I learned about texture from them and about attitude, particularly. The attitude [of the era] is something you really have to grasp. You have to take lessons in a sense, build it, coach what is really right. How you represent yourself—it's more than the costumes, what you take from attics. Today, if kids [rebel] against the parents it's their job! Another thing today, kids and their parents, they're certain about themselves. [Today's kids] are more definite, more confident. But back then [this confidence] was just becoming [true], so you have to get them not so certain about what they're saying in order to provide that attitude and make the period correct.

Filmmaker: How was it working with the casts of these last two films?

Lee: It was very different. Somehow Americans were brought up more with movies. At least with this group, [Americans] were more comfortable with the camera, the way of looking when they're being observed. They're more natural and more comfortable. I think they're more used to the idea of movie stars. British performers, it's hard to get the camera around them or observe them in some obscure place where they feel all naked and uncomfortable. It's weird acting. They choose what they want you to see. If they're not in control, they're nervous. Compared to the Americans, it's harder to get the simple, innocent but moving moments from British actors. I always end up confusing them instead of convincing them to get it.

Filmmaker: Do you try to keep the actors a little bit uncomfortable, on the edge?

Lee: That's important. If they're comfortable doing a scene, it's not right.

It starts from the very beginning, from the first rehearsal. You say, "God, this is the hardest thing I've ever played." Whatever you do is wrong. To keep a balance is a sort of Zen approach. Whatever you do is the thing you need to deconstruct.

Filmmaker: You've made *The Ice Storm* at a time when the subject of families is not being addressed by American movies.
Schamus: I wouldn't know. Having kids, I see so few of them.

Filmmaker: Well, if you only see the ones you produce, you see a lot.
Schamus: I've seen *The Little Mermaid* about five thousand times. Having been exposed ad nauseam to Disney films, you begin to realize that what passes for family entertainment is virulently Oedipal. Most Disney movies begin with the murder of one or more parent, whether it's *Bambi* or *The Lion King*. To be a parent in a Disney movie is to be viewed through the scope of a very powerful viewfinder attached to some very powerful artillery!

Filmmaker: How do you see the connections between the families in this film and the families in the Taiwanese films? One thing that struck me is that *The Ice Storm* takes place in an area that's not dissimilar from the place where the guys in *Pushing Hands* live.
Lee: It's different.

Filmmaker: What's the difference?
Lee: [New Canaan, Connecticut] is more advanced, more civilized. I don't mean [in terms of] behavior, but the civilization is looking ahead. It's more liberated.

Filmmaker: It seems like the cultures of the two films are almost opposite in some ways. That the Chinese, the problems come from obsessive conformity and obedience to authority and tradition. Whereas in America, in this period especially, there are more problems associated with being rebellious and too liberated.
Lee: Exactly. What moved me was not "the sixties." It wasn't the student movement. This [film depicts] the hangover of the sixties. It finally sunk in to the quiet, middle class. The structure is shaking, the world's collapsing.

Filmmaker: Were you in Taiwan when all this was going on? Were you in high school at this time?

Lee: The first year [of high school] was a pivotal year for me. I studied to get into college to honor my father and mother. And I blew the college examination that year! My father was the principle of the high school. That was a big turning point for me. I got into the Academy of Arts. And from the first time I stood on stage, that was it. I knew what I wanted to do.

Filmmaker: James, do you come from a John Cheever background?

Schamus: No, I grew up in L.A. When I was an English grad at Berkeley, reading Updike and Cheever was the equivalent of drinking dry martinis at the country club.

Filmmaker: I want to ask the two of you about your working relationship. It's unusual in the sense that James is both a writer and producer, and this is a long term thing. It's not just one film. How does that relationship work?

Lee: Usually, when you read scripts they're written for studio executives. They're built like a battleship to prove that the work doesn't leave a lot of room for the filmmaker. But Jim doesn't do that to me. What can you do cinematically that's exciting? It's that kind of relationship. It's a lot of fun. I'm lucky. I'd probably make different movies without James. Even in the Chinese movies, he'll give me another perspective.

Filmmaker: James, what have you learned as a screenwriter from working with Ang?

Schamus: You have to think of screenwriting as writing for somebody else. I have to think of it as a job. If I have to write a screenplay to satisfy myself, it would be the biggest piece of trash. Luckily, my primary audience is Ang, not "the American people" or Peter Guber. I have an audience, and it's a guy who knows what he's up to.

Filmmaker: Now, people want to know where a film is going to end up within the first five minutes. This film violates that in a major way.

Schamus: I'm pleased we could do that and keep people with us. We were taking that from movies of the seventies like the Paul Mazursky stuff, *Bob & Carol & Ted & Alice*. It will never make it into the auteurist pantheon but this is amazing stuff. Another true oddity: *The Swimmer*, with Burt Lancaster. He's in his Speedos the whole movie!

Ride with the Devil: Ang Lee Interview

Ellen Kim / 1999

From Hollywood.com, October 8, 1999. Reprinted by permission.

It was about time Ang Lee took on the Civil War.

After films such as *Eat Drink Man Woman*, *Sense and Sensibility*, and *The Ice Storm*, which explored love and family feuds, it seems only natural Lee would take on a national feud. This time he helms the war epic *Ride with the Devil*, opening November 24 in New York and Los Angeles.

Lee, who was born and raised in Taiwan but studied theater and film in the States, drew initial acclaim for his Taiwan-based "Father Knows Best" trilogy: *Pushing Hands*, *The Wedding Banquet*, and *Eat Drink Man Woman*. The latter two films received Best Foreign-Language Film nominations at the Academy Awards and Golden Globes in 1992 and 1994.

When the call came for his first U.S. project, 1995's sisterly romance *Sense and Sensibility*, Lee says he was surprised at the material. "They thought I could do Jane Austen," Lee said with a chuckle. "There was Emma Thompson, so I couldn't resist—[but] I was totally scared. My first time doing an English-language film and it's Jane Austen."

But the film was reviewed as one of the year's best, racking up Oscar and Golden Globe nominations. Although Lee was denied a nod for Best Director, the film and stars Thompson and Kate Winslet were nominated, and Thompson took home a trophy for Best Adapted Screenplay. Says Lee, "I think after that I only wanted to do period pieces."

His next U.S. film catapulted him to another period altogether, a middle-class American suburbia in the 1970s, for 1997's *The Ice Storm*, a drama about family and sexual awakening. The film, starring Kevin Kline, Sigourney Weaver, Joan Allen, and Christina Ricci, was critically lauded but virtually ignored at awards time, and Lee looked to his next project.

"I'm always looking forward to something bigger," Lee said. "I think I pretty much said what I want to say about family drama. I think I won't do family drama for at least a long while."

Ride with the Devil, based on Daniel Woodrell's 1987 novel *Woe to Live On*, bounces Lee to another place and time: the Kansas-Missouri border during the Civil War. A group of pro-Southern young men called Bushwhackers adds two new members, childhood friends Jake (Tobey Maguire) and Jack Bull (Skeet Ulrich). As the war rages on, the pair encounter enemies from the North and within their unit, and find love in the form of a young widow (pop singer Jewel).

The film is less an epic about war than a character study about outsiders changed by war. For the lead roles, the studios were pursuing Leonardo DiCaprio and Matt Damon, but Lee, who worked with Maguire in *The Ice Storm*, knew he was the one for the character of Jake when he read the book.

"I can never get tired of watching this guy," Lee said of Maguire. "People say the lead character sometimes is the director himself. I found he has a lot of myself: passive, observant—which is hard to make into a leading man. You can watch him change in a situation, be observant and you fall for him. And he has a demeanor that looks very believable. Most actors I work with don't necessarily believe in the part that they play. But he does—with his whole body. I think he's a director's dream."

Another character who required precise casting was Holt, a loyal former slave of a Bushwhacker who becomes Jake's friend and confidant but doesn't speak for the first half of the film.

"When I read the book, that character was the first one that caught my attention, that I identify with," Lee said. "For years I was a foreigner here. . . . There's this thing about liberation and emancipation, but what moves me so much [was] his self-awareness . . . self-emancipation. The story is not really about the Civil War. The subtext is about civil rights, so that coming-of-age story really moves me."

Jeffrey Wright (*Basquiat*) was the first actor Lee auditioned for the role of Holt, and the director said he stuck in his mind.

"I liked his eyes—I think his eyes captured me," Lee said. "You think, what is he thinking. I think they had a beautiful quality; [he had a] beautiful voice. Plus, he's a good actor."

Lee is currently shooting *Crouching Tiger, Hidden Dragon*, an action film set in nineteenth-century China, another new direction for him.

"Doing a martial-arts film [is] something I always wanted to do. I don't want to be pigeonholed; I want to grow as a filmmaker," Lee said. "To me, this whole career is like a big film school. . . . And this time I do a connection to the previous film, like relationship or social obligation vs. personal freedom and changing times. Just taking bigger strides."

Ang Lee and James Schamus

Neil Norman / 2000

From the *Guardian*, November 7, 2000. Interview conducted at the British Film Institute. Copyright Guardian News and Media Ltd. 2000. Reprinted by permission.

Neil Norman: Let's start with *Crouching Tiger, Hidden Dragon*. This is based on the fourth of a five-part novel sequence, a sort of Chinese pulp fiction. At what stage did you see the possibility of a film within this?

Ang Lee: I read the book through a friend of mine who knew I was a fan of this particular writer in 1994. The fourth volume, which is the story of a young girl, Jen, struck me that there was a movie there. When there is a strong woman character in a story—that always grabs me. Especially in this very macho genre, which since boyhood I've wanted to do. It felt as if it took six movies for me to even begin to earn the right to make this kind of movie. Of course, I'm growing up, I'm an established filmmaker, known for making family dramas about personal relationships, I cannot go all the way and make a purely genre film, I've got to throw everything I know into the movie—like a combination platter. The key is to keep the balance.

I think the book struck me in a few ways that I thought very interesting to pick it as my first martial arts film. It has a very strong female character and it was very abundant in classic Chinese textures. Usually these pulp fiction books are set aside from the lawful society—they create a world called Giang Hu, which is an entanglement, a relationship with the underworld, with swordsmanship—almost like a fairytale. But this one is not quite that way, it is very abundant in what I care about—and also to do with the process of Chinese history, which has been lost, classic Chinese textures, which I know from history, my parents, from movies. It gives the impression of China which is kind of like the hidden dragon in me, in some ways, and I feel I want to pursue it.

At the same time I was offered *Sense and Sensibility*—I couldn't refuse that job, it was just too good a job—so I made that. Meanwhile, *The Ice Storm* was still in development. And that was something I really wanted to do, and frankly I don't think I was ready to do a big production like this. Then I did another movie, *Ride with the Devil*, and then I thought I was ready. Going back after three major league productions, English-language films, including one somewhat action film, *Ride with the Devil*, I thought I was ready. I was, you know, tougher. And then James can tell you about the scripting process. There's the script and financing. Meanwhile, I went to Beijing and started to do location scouting. It's a process of two years. Five, six months of pre-production, then five months of shooting and five months of post-production and then seven or eight months in promotions.

NN: The remarkable thing about this being a Chinese production is that there are resonant myths with the west. For example, the Green Destiny sword can be compared to Excalibur in Arthurian legend. And there seem to be bits of Hamlet dotted all over the film. Was this embedded in the text itself, or was it something you drew out in order to make it more universal?

AL: I think people are universal. I took the name Green Destiny from— well there is such a sword called Green Destiny. It is green because you keep twisting it, it's an ancient skill, you keep twisting it and knocking it and twisting it until it is very elastic and light. Swoosh! It swings like that, you know?

Green Destiny is a name which is derived from the book, and I took the name and I go further with the Taoist philosophy. The jade fox— the old green, the murky green that's what the green really means. It is the ultimate yin-ness. Yin and yang where everything exists in and derives from . . . this is hard to explain. The most mysterious feminine factor, the existence that we men, we don't know. It's woman. It's feminine. That's what the sword is about. That's the symbolic meaning of the sword. Even in Chinese you probably don't get that . . . I don't know. But that's for me. Anything green is hidden dragon, desires and repression . . . something weird when you dig into the depth. I think there is something like that in Excalibur, for example . . .

We didn't exactly have that in mind for a western audience. For a western audience, I think between James and me, the bouncing back and forth between Chinese and English, I think it is a good exercise to make it reasonable for a worldwide audience—not just a western audience— a worldwide audience and to some degree a modern Chinese audience as well. Things and logic that we used to take for granted in the Orient might not be that logical today. It's a good example—how to tell a story with a global sense. That means more layout of the texture of society, more explanation of rules of the games. For example, the first fight does not ensue until fifteen minutes into the movie. To a Chinese audience it must feel like thirty minutes—"Are we gonna see a fight or what?" Usually with this genre the first thing that happens is a good fight sequence to show that you're in good hands. So we broke that rule. I think a lot of that comes from the western audience.

I also didn't want to make just a martial arts film, you know, there's drama in it. I think there is somewhat of a western three-act structure that lays things out. Starting with a crisis or an action, things like that, or verbalizing a relationship.

NN: James, I know you've worked on all of Ang's scripts, aside from *Sense and Sensibility*, but you've worked on all of Ang's films. But never anything like this. What sort of a challenge was it for you to tackle the stunt aspect of the script?

JS: It was an amazing challenge, because in fact I didn't do it. [Laughter] On the first draft of the script I had a little preamble. As you go through the scenes and get to the fight scene, I remember exactly the language I used—"They fight." The preamble said, "While I fail to explain the fight scenes, I can assure you that they will be the greatest fight scenes ever written in cinema history. Period." And that was our pitch to the distributors we were selling the film to at that time. I knew two things. One was that Ang was going to insist on crafting fight sequences that were not simply the kind of western fight sequences where there's a bad guy who wants to kill the good guy, while the good guy doesn't really want to kill the bad guy—but in the fight the bad guy gets the upper hand, and it looks like the good guy's going to die, but at the last minute the good guy kills the bad guy. Only he doesn't kill the bad guy, he just disables him, then the bad guy finally gets out of the tub with the knife and the good guy has to kill him. [Laughter]

So I knew that they were going to be expressions of relationships and meaningful. Because in most of the fights in this movie, one person really doesn't want to fight. So it's a really interesting situation, having to make dramatic fight scenes when they are more or less than that. So I knew that Ang, and in particular our martial arts choreographer, Yuen Woo-Ping, would work all this stuff out on set in pre-production. It's one of those great ironies that when we mention Yuen Woo-Ping over here in the west it's always suffixed by "of *The Matrix* fame." Because he did do the choreography for *The Matrix*, which we loved, but of course we know him as the guy who created Jackie Chan's career and Jet Li's career. And it's amazing to see thirty years later, full circle, the cultures revolving, and so Yuen Woo-Ping returns to us as the guy who did *The Matrix*.

NN: As the film was being put together, there were reports about the different castings. I gather that Jet Li was in fact considered for the main role and I understand that you were planning two language versions—one in English and one in Mandarin. Is that true?

AL: That was just a thought. Is it doable? I don't know. Has anyone done it before? I don't know. It seemed to be a waste of time to shoot two versions. Am I going to direct them with equal intensity? All of the actors had better Chinese than English. Are they going to struggle with their English? Production-wise it doesn't make sense. Unless there were, like, fifty lines in the movie, then maybe I could manage to do that. But there are too many lines in the movie. So I decided not to do that and stick with Mandarin.

Yeah, Jet Li, the first thing you think about when doing a martial arts film is him. But at that time it was a much smaller project, I really intended to make the movie as *Sense and Sensibility* with martial arts [laughs] . . . a two woman story. . . . So the men are just generally supporting roles, just a touch, just a vehicle for their romance and conflict. So Jet Li was invited . . . but it didn't work out. . . .

Anyway, Chow Yun-Fat was the next big movie star. I don't see that as a Jackie Chan part. [Laughter] Chow Yun-Fat said he will never play a period piece. Will never shave his head and have a ponytail. He's never held a sword before. But I know he's a good actor, and drop-dead gorgeous and everything, so I show him the script and, at that stage, he is willing to take the job. So I was very moved. So he is not going to do tumbling and all kinds of fantastic Jet Li–styles of fighting, so the fighting gets reduced and his part gets really beefed-up. His relation with Michelle Yeoh really gets beefed up, and the part really becomes a romantic lead. I think, thinking back, we were lucky to have him. The movie is more a romantic drama.

NN: So the fact that you cast him changed the emotional weight of the movie?

AL: Yes. I always do that. Sometimes it happens in the writing, sometimes in the directing. Like Zhang Zi-Yi, the young girl, she didn't turn out to be the way I see the part, so I have to veer the movie towards her and make it work. I think I am the actors' tailor. As far as casting is concerned, until the last moment of the music is composed, the job is not done. The whole process is casting. You have to make them look like they're perfectly cast.

NN: Your last four films have been based on novels. Rick Moody's *The Ice Storm*, Austen's *Sense and Sensibility*, and Daniel Woodrell's book *Woe to Live On*, and now this. When you have a source material to work from, do you think in a different way when you approach the script? James?
JS: Oh, me?

NN: Well, both of you. . . . [Laughter]
AL: It's running out of things to write about. That's why I adapt. . . .
JS: Well essentially it means I can get away with a first draft just by ripping off somebody else. . . . [Laughter] Which is a great comfort. Because that first stage is just going through and underlining all the juicy bits and then trying to run them in some kind of order that makes sense cinematically. Then the hard part actually does take over, and you realize that novels don't simply translate into movies. Assuming that the world the novel created for you is the basis for the enjoyment of the script and the film is a deadly error. Because that world doesn't exist once you're dealing in cinematic terms—you have to create it every step of the way. It's like film production itself.

My partner Ted Hope, at Good Machine, who started as an assistant director, the guy who ran the set, used to say it's like a Phillip K. Dick novel, if you don't think about the floor, it's not there and you fall through it. And to a certain extent it's the same adapting novels, you suddenly realize you've forgotten what you need to do to make it into a movie. So it's an interesting process, it's a good process for lazy people, because the first stage is so easy, and it's a good process for procrastinators, because you already have a draft before you even start thinking about making a movie.

NN: Does this mean that we're not going to have any more original Ang Lee scripts?
AL: There could be an original James Schamus script. . . . I don't care about writing really. When I started out, nobody gave me scripts, so I had to write. . . . That's why I wrote family drama—I'm a domestic person, it's all I know! Now I'm kind of established as a director, I much prefer

directing to writing. Writing's lonely. Directing, I get all kinds of inspiration. It's working with people. It's a lot more fun. When I have a full schedule like that, I don't see myself sitting there for a couple of months, doing the research, going through a painful process, it's just not my thing anymore. I grab the life I have to direct as many movies as I can.

NN: Let's look at that early stage, about 1985. You were at NYU film school, you had a couple of scripts, you were not being able to get films made. So you sent two scripts into a competition run by the Taiwanese government. These scripts were *Pushing Hands*, which won the first prize, and *The Wedding Banquet*, which won second prize. Not a bad way to start! That gave you the impetus to get a film made. Enter Good Machine, James's company. How did that meeting of minds come about?
AL: When I sent those scripts, that was the lowest point of my life. We'd just had our second son, and when I went to collect them from hospital, I went to the bank to try and get some money to buy some diapers, the screen showed I've got $26 left. Terrible. Anyway, my first Chinese script was *The Wedding Banquet*, it was written six years before it was made into a film. At that time making a Chinese-language film in America was inconceivable, no one would give me money, no matter how small it was. And it was gay-related subject matter, so I couldn't raise the money in Taiwan either, so it just sat there.

Then at the end of 1989 a friend of mine saw an advert that that year they were expanding the script competition to off-sea Chinese. The top award was equivalent to $16,000—good money. I had this idea of *Pushing Hands* and the old Tai-Chi master for a long time but I never wanted to write it. I felt like in that six years I was sitting there like an old Tai-Chi master at home, going nowhere. [Laughter]

I never meant to make that movie, but I know that if I write that movie I can win the top prize from the Taiwanese government. So I wrote it for the sake of the competition. So I won it, and they sent me a ticket to receive the prize in Taiwan. So when I arrive, they say, the studio, that they want to make three movies. It's related to the government, called Central Motion Pictures, and it had just changed management. They say they want to make three movies, one is going to be done by a new director, we know we're going to lose money so just do what you want. [Laughter] "The American wife in that part? Just don't choose anyone too ugly." [Laughter]

A third of the budget was funded by the government, a third is a video package deal they had, so there's only equivalent to $100,000 investment, so they said go ahead and do it. The story was set in New York, and I took the money, but I said, "Give me a couple of days, I dunno if I want to do it." I'd been waiting ten years. . . . I didn't want to make a flop. Anyway, I took the money and I was looking for a line producer, and through a friend of mine I knew Ted. And then there was Ted and James at the new-found Good Machine. They shared two tables with another company, I think. So I did my pitch. And they did their pitch. They told me that they were the kings of no-budget filmmaking in New York. [Laughter]

James looked like a used-car salesman and a professor. . . . And they said, "Pay attention. We said 'no-budget' not 'low-budget.' Your money, about $400,000. . . .

JS: 350.

AL: "$350,000 is luxury for us." They offered something very tempting to me. They said they were director-centered producers. They wanted to teach the directors how to make the movies that they can afford instead of spending time in development hell—and I'd just spent six years in there . . . so I know how that tastes. And over the years I'm just glad that these two guys, I'm just glad they're not crooks! [Laughter]

And they did keep their promise. They did grow together with me and they still teach me how to make the movie I can afford. All the movies you see—small ones, bigger ones—they fumble along the way like I do. They're learning how to deal with bigger people and different situations, international money-raising and sales. The first movie, *Pushing Hands*, didn't make any money except in Taiwan, so James said, "Let me help you with the script for the second one." And that hit. *The Wedding Banquet* was international, and we were capable of doing one after another, Chinese, English. . . . It is a very fruitful and nurturing relationship that we get to grow together. I now want them to teach me how to make *Terminator 3*. . . .

Questions from the Audience

Q: You appear to leap from genre to genre; do you program those leaps into the development stage?

JS: Looking for some juicy new genre to attack? It hasn't necessarily been problematic, but I think there's two things that have happened as the years go by. One related to the nerd side of me, which is an engagement with the film's historical record and the traditions, and many of them are Hollywood traditions that Hollywood itself has just forgotten as the fads pile up. I think the engagement with that, those tasks, is very enriching for me personally. For Ang it's a different tack, but it's also quite similar, to rub up against those traditions, to continually test your craft, to treat yourself as a craftsperson as well as an artist. There's a certain luxury associated with that exercise. So I think that the generic imperative is going to continue, we don't necessarily have one that we're dying to do next. Although musicals have been bandied around a bit. . . . [Laughter] But we haven't really decided yet.

AL: That's the beauty of working with James, I think, a film professor. You know, whenever I am tired of doing this one, abundant sources come my way. Swoosh! So writing the script is the least interesting thing to us. It's what film we're going to create, what fun we're going to have, what kind of angle are we going to put on it, what juice are we going to put in. That was the real fun, not genre or script writing—you know, craft, what fun we're going to have.

Q: *Crouching Tiger, Hidden Dragon* seems to be a big leap of faith. What was the danger? The financial risk?

AL: Of course it was a big risk. A lot of stress. It was something I've wanted to do for a long time, but didn't really have the skill until I'd made six films. Then I was ready to take the challenge. I think the biggest challenge I had was doing a genre film that takes a lot of money to make, and on top of that I want to make A-grade drama, and see if I can keep a balance and have both of them benefit each other. On top of that, I want to do a big landscape in China. So all of that is very challenging. To me it is important after three English-language films that I go back to my cultural roots, to fulfill my boyhood dreams. But it also a new adventure, because that kind of filmmaking is low budget in America but is titanic in China. There are no rules. We get to make the rules. There's no producer to look over my shoulder. There is no set standard. Of course, I keep testing the limit.

James will tell you the story of how much each area would give for an Ang Lee film with Chow Yun-Fat and Michelle Yeoh. Then they would give us a number and we would come up with that budget. James can fill you in. It's a very interesting process, the financial process, and what's at stake. Once the money's raised, we're OK, we're making the movie. But for the investors, the movie has to make $60 million to break even. No Chinese film has ever come close to that. It's a kind of mission impossible. But it's what we want to do.

JS: Well, these were interesting circumstances to go asking for money in Hollywood for Ang for a Chinese-language film. Namely because after the "blockbuster" success of *The Ice Storm* and the "firestorm of praise and heaps of money" that showered upon us after *Ride with the Devil*. . . . Basically, if this film didn't work, Ang would be directing segments for Fox TV's *Scariest Animal Moments* . . . so there was a little bit of iffyness involved. And the Taiwanese billionaire who pledged to put up all the money, I don't know, maybe it was a bad mahjong day or something. . . .

AL: It was the Asian economic storm. . . .

JS: The virus. Anyhow. So we had to pull numbers out of Europe, and particularly a lot of long-standing friends and the distribution community here, who still had faith in Ang, and prove with those numbers that this film could support a budget of X dollars. At that point we brought in Sony Pictures Classics in the States, another Sony—the Columbia Pictures, Asia, and then the Sony entity of Columbia Pictures International in order to pick up the other territories, including the Asian territories and Latin America. There was this corporate family who came in to put the pieces together and help us make the film. But at that point it was also a corporate family whose cookie jar was empty. So we had to bank all these contracts, we had to find a bank that was crazy enough to do that, and that was in France. Then we had to get a bond company to insure the movie, because the bank wouldn't give us any money until we had an insurance policy that said we would deliver this wacky movie that was being shot all over China. So they were in Los Angeles. And then we had the Taiwanese production end. But in order to close the deals, for tax reasons (it's a complicated story), they had to set up a subsidiary in the British Virgin Islands. Our limited liability corporation, that we set up in the United States, had the sub-license to English-language rights. So we ended up with literally thousands of pages of legal documentation, all of which had to be signed in a circular way—one of those things where the guy in Italy isn't going to sign until the guy in France has signed. Meanwhile they were in Beijing already, pre-producing the movie and more or less mortgaging Ang's house. So it was a little iffy.

NN: All of which could have been put at risk by one or two tiny accidents, like Michelle Yeoh messing up her knee quite early on in the shoot?

AL: Yes, second week of shooting, unfortunately. Doing a spinning flying-kick, something she did thousands of times. But she didn't pay attention and it was at the end of a night's shooting, and "crack," she snapped her knee ligament and has to be sent away for surgery. For about two and a half months we have to reschedule everything. It was a nightmare. The movie started out shooting in the Gobi desert—it was just a logistical nightmare—sandstorms, lost in the desert and flood. In the desert. Two weeks of rain! [Laughter]

JS: The locals went up to our producer, Bill Kong, who had been burning incense each day for good luck and getting none of it. They said, "Thank you so much for burning that incense, because that's what we do when we want rain!"

AL: So the whole production was like that. Nothing worked. Every little detail I had to, like, kill myself, kill everybody, just to make it work. The whole production was like that. I thought I was dying sometimes. I don't know how I lived through that. When people ask me about a sequel . . . [Laughter] It's just insane.

Q: Is the novel of *Crouching Tiger, Hidden Dragon* available here?

JS: We're trying to arrange it . . . well, there was an abridged version of the novel published in Taiwan and they're trying to arrange a translation of that abridged version. Of course, that abridged version was copyright piracy . . . oh yeah . . . so, who knows if they'll cut through that.

Q: Are you both fans of the martial arts genre, and if so, which are your favorite directors in the genre?

AL: I grew up with it. I'm a big fan. When I was younger it's the storytelling that really grabbed me, the fantasy storytelling, about power, about personal transcendence, about romance. Morality tales. A secret joy we had when growing up. As I grew a little older, the Hong Kong choreographers took over the genre and made fantastic fight sequences. Of course, they don't really care what's in between the fights. So that film language really fascinated me as a young film student. So it really fascinated me in both ways. I really wanted to hit the high notes of the Hong Kong action standards, while I have the fantastic movie and the applause and everything else. So that's something I've always wanted to do.

Among those directors, King Hu is more of a director to look up to, and Chang Cheh is one of them. The recent ones, they don't really influence me except some of the really classic fighting sequences—the stories I didn't care for much.

JS: I saw a fair amount when we were researching the film. My current favorite is Chang Cheh, who was working in the sixties and seventies, and if you ever get the chance to score a tape of *One-Armed Swordsman*. . . . These are incredibly brutal, queer, kind of sadomasochistic fight movies, with all these greased-up guys chopping each other to bits. They're pretty fun! [Laughter]

Q: I heard you were planning a prequel next year, and also is it true that Chow Yun-Fat has declared that he is taking a break from film for the next year and a half?

JS: If I were Chow and had made this movie with this guy—I wouldn't work again.

AL: Not next year. I couldn't take it anymore. I'm so exhausted. I probably need to make one or two English-language films to recover from it. Physically I can't take it anymore.

JS: But don't worry, they'll be twenty other Chinese movies with the title *Crouching Tiger, Hidden Dragon—the Prequel,* coming out next year. . . .

Q: You portray very interesting female characters in your movies. You don't see that very often in films, so where do you get your ideas from?

AL: From my wife, I suppose. Seriously. And my ex-girlfriend. Actually I was brought up in a very chauvinist, traditional Chinese male way, but at heart I guess I'm just not a macho guy. I'm not going to be John Woo. Strong women attract me in real life, and in dramatic context. A strong woman, when her heart is broken, it breaks my heart. It's something that speaks for me very well. When there are such characters in the text, I just tend to grab them. I don't know why. It's just chemistry. I find that I do a much better job with strong female characters than anything else.

Somehow in Asia, I notice, women make up 80 per cent of my audience. So you see women with crouching men sitting next to them [pulls the face of a very quiet, small man], maybe at *The Wedding Banquet* you'll see a couple of guys.

I think it is also a refreshing angle to check into repressed male-dominated society. Particularly for this one, which is a very macho genre, it just gives a different angle. There is a deeper emotional depth because we are taking an emotional tour with the heroines. I just like that. It's the best thing I can offer, I suppose.

Q: Could you speak about the fight sequence in the forest at the end of the movie—how long did it take?

AL: It took two weeks to shoot that scene. Most of it is on the editing floor. . . . It was just a crazy idea that I had and everyone refused to do it for months. There is no shortage of sword fighting in bamboo forests, because bamboo provides a very romantic environment. In China, bamboo symbolizes righteousness—it shoots straight up, it's elastic, like the swordsmanship. Also it provides a very interesting foreground. But normally no one ever gets up there because it's undo-able. That's why I wanted to do it.

The color of green is really the Hidden Dragon for me in the movie, against the color of red in the desert flashback. The crouching one, the forbidden one to me is really green. The Green Destiny, Jade-eyed Fox. Anything green, with a little bit of white, is very sexy and taboo-ish for me. So I thought the bamboo-choreographed sequence really, in an abstract way, is mesmerizing. It's not really a fight. I thought it was a good place to do it. You know, we live in a place with gravity. I sort of underestimate that.

It's very painful for the actors and I worry about their safety. They were down in the bamboo forest in the southern part of China, in the valleys. It's hard to get a big construction crane in there. We managed to get four or five in there and hang the actors up. There's the valley and the creek, so they're really high up there, and we had to build platforms for the tighter shots. Once you cut the bamboo, the leaves dwindle. Only on drizzling days can you shoot for half an hour, then you have to change the bamboo again. It's really painful. But it's a crazy idea.

Q: I wasn't really sure about the flashback scenes. Why did you spend so long in the desert when it didn't seem to be crucial to the film? And also, how does scriptwriting work in terms of there having to be a constant translation between English and Chinese?

JS: I can answer the first question about the flashback: It's a big mistake, we're sorry. [Laughter] It was a very big topic for us. In general, every time I see the movie, which is less and less (but he [Ang Lee] sits through it all the time!) I think, "I can't believe we got away with this!" All of a sudden, for twenty minutes, they go back there . . . and it's completely unapologetic, it's like cut/back, cut/back. We're ready to take it on the chin a bit, hence my feistiness. But there are a lot of reasons why we love the flashback.

But I'll tell you a little about the scriptwriting process. It was extremely educational for me, and extremely painful for Ang. We started with a Chinese-language draft, and then Ang made a précis of the parts of the fourth volume that were most important to him. Then I wrote this completely entertaining swash-buckling romantic adventurous epic movie, that was a joke to the Chinese who read it. I use the analogy that if a Chinese person wrote a John Wayne western, and he rides into town, gets off his horse, walks over to the sheriff, says "Howdy" and then, like, kow-tows nine times. . . . [Laughter]

But the structure was there. I think if I was Chinese it would be a nightmare parody of my entire culture. But structurally, I think, it still ended up working. Then Ang and Hui-Ling Wang really took it over and from inside-out really transformed the film, and really got into a lot of the cultural references, indices—the soul, which I had misread. Even though I'd read a lot of Chinese stuff in English translation and seen a lot of movies, I misread almost every cue. So it was great that the process became six months of mutual torture through bad translation. . . . Can you imagine trying to write your script and have somebody who had been fired from the UN doing bad translation? . . . I always thought we were going to make a movie that was understandable to westerners, but still very Chinese, and I still think essentially it's a Chinese film. But in a way I also recognize that why the film has been so massively successful in Asia is not because it retained its Asian identity, but because of all these wonderful new things that came about in discourse with the West. Especially in regards to the female characters and the romance, which are very foreign to the genre. I think that one of the things I find people responding to here in the West is precisely the fact that you get to see a two-hour Taoist action movie. The Chinese-ness of it, even if it's not always entirely comprehensible because of the subtitles, I think that's what's so profoundly new about it. So in a way we ended up making an eastern movie for western audiences and in some ways a more western movie for eastern audiences.

AL: To me, James is the best writer I personally know of. Take this film, it has to hit Asia like a summer blockbuster, but at the same time it has to be in the art-house cinemas and the New York Film Festival. So from the New York Film Festival to Asian blockbuster is a big range to cover. James doesn't know Chinese, but the structure and the film logic and the sellability, marketability, and the pure grade of how good the script is. I do need his help, that's just the bottom line. It's painful for me to say so, but Goddamn it, it's so true.

Q: I just have a comment, not a question. I found *Crouching Tiger, Hidden Dragon* exhilarating and profoundly moving. I want to say thank you.
NN: I've seen it twice and I think it's the most amazing film I've seen in a long time. Thank you, James Schamus and Ang Lee.

Enter the Dragon

David E. Williams / 2001

From *American Cinematographer* 82, no. 1 (January 2001). Reprinted by permission.

Few modern filmmakers have mastered the use of characters and story as fully as writer/director Ang Lee. Over the course of just seven feature films, he has established himself as a cinematic chameleon capable of exploring widely varied time periods and social structures to create dramas of substance.

Born and raised in Taiwan, Lee moved to the United States in 1978 to attend the University of Illinois, where he received a bachelor's degree in theater. He later earned a master's degree in film from New York University. In 1992, he directed his first feature, *Pushing Hands*, which began a fruitful collaboration with screenwriter/producer James Schamus that continues to this day.

Pushing Hands, which focuses on the familial bonds of a Chinese family living in Manhattan, became the first film in Lee's "Father Knows Best Trilogy" along with *The Wedding Banquet* (1993) and *Eat Drink Man Woman* (1994, see *AC* Jan. '95). Each picture illustrates the strained roles of love, family, and tradition within modern Asian society, and each earned critical kudos for the director.

Despite these successes with dramatic storytelling, Lee surprised some filmgoers with *Sense and Sensibility*, the 1995 adaptation of Jane Austen's classic tale of a love that's nearly thwarted by social mores. The film's fresh spirit—fostered in no small part by Michael Coulter, BSC's Oscar-nominated cinematography (see *AC* June '96)—found favor with audiences. In 1996, Lee again changed course with *The Ice Storm* (see *AC* Oct. '97), his first feature on an entirely American subject: family values (or the lack thereof) in the bleak, bourgeois landscape of 1970s America. Unfortunately, the subtle brilliance of this picture, which featured stark, moody camerawork by Frederick Elmes, ASC, was lost on many.

Lee returned in 1999 with the Civil War–era Western *Ride with the Devil*. Shot in widescreen anamorphic by Elmes (see *AC* Nov. '99), this picture once again illustrated the director's ability to weave complex characters through a compelling drama.

Now, in another move that confounds convention, Lee has returned with *Crouching Tiger, Hidden Dragon*, an astonishing take on the martial-arts genre that won critical and popular raves during its debut at last year's Cannes Film Festival.

AC spoke to Lee before and after the premiere of *Crouching Tiger* at Cannes, and the conversations ranged from the specifics of making the movie in China to his boyhood love of bone-crunching kung fu films.

American Cinematographer: How were you introduced to the book upon which *Crouching Tiger* is based?

Ang Lee: I'm an admirer of the novelist, Wang Dulu, who wrote a lot of martial-arts fiction—which was very popular when I was growing up in Taiwan. Most of this genre is pulp fiction, but *Crouching Tiger* was something else: even though the characters could fly, [the story] was grounded in reality. Usually, the female characters [in such tales] are very passive; here the main woman was very active and very rebellious. That made it very interesting.

This novel was written just before World War II, and about five years ago a good friend of mine brought it to my attention. I've been wanting to make the film since then. After *The Ice Storm*, I decided that after making three films in English, I had to make a Chinese film. This story had stayed with me over the years, and I had wanted to make a martial-arts film since boyhood.

AC: Can you elaborate on the story and how its focus on female characters makes it different?

Lee: The martial-arts genre is traditionally very macho, but [this film has] two very important female leads, played by Michelle Yeoh and Zhang Ziyi. They are the anchors of the movie, and although other martial-arts films have strong female characters, they are not usually the focus of the story. Whether this is because of the material, the filmmakers, or the intended audience, I don't know.

AC: What were some of the reasons for making the film in the Mandarin language?

Lee: Well, this was my boyhood fantasy and a piece of martial-arts fiction, so I had to make it a Chinese-language film. I just didn't know how it would look and sound to me if it were in English—for me, that would be like seeing John Wayne speaking Chinese in a Western! Maybe the market for the film won't be as broad as it could have been [if it were in English], but we wanted to keep the fantasy elements working, so perhaps the foreign language will work better for some viewers. There are people flying through the air and doing all kinds of stunts, and maybe audiences will accept those things better.

AC: I know that the writing of this script was a complicated process. The story for the film is just one segment of the novel; in addition, one of the screenwriters, James Schamus, who also produced the film, doesn't read Chinese, and there is no English translation of the novel.

Lee: James has worked on all of my films since *The Wedding Banquet*, so we're pals and fellow filmmakers—I never treat him like [just] a screenwriter! In this case, when we were raising money, he did the first draft of the script, basing his work on a scenario that I had written from the novel, which is very long. Hui-Ling Wang, who worked with us on *Eat Drink Man Woman*, did the second draft, and he was pretty much starting from scratch because he was writing in Chinese. We went back and forth on that a few times, with me as the "in between" person. There were a lot of other challenges on this film, such as trying to bring high drama to what is essentially a B-movie action story, as well as bringing Hollywood production standards to a Chinese film made in China.

AC: What type of working relationship did you have with your cinematographer, Peter Pau, who has extensive experience in making martial-arts fantasy films? Did he help you to capture the authentic flavor you were after?

Lee: Peter is probably the biggest and most Hollywood-like cinematographer in all of Hong Kong. In fact, he's probably more Hollywood in style than Fred Elmes [ASC], who shot my last two films, *The Ice Storm* and *Ride with the Devil*. Peter has made several big martial-arts films, such as *The Bride with White Hair*, [as well as] some very artistic films. He's also done a lot of action work, and he's made some films in Hollywood. He brought the best crew with him, he operated the camera, and he worked with us on the budget by helping us get the equipment we needed for five months—Peter means a lot to the rental houses in Hong Kong! He has directed films, and he even served as our assistant director—he's probably one of the few cinematographers in the world who can do all of that. What else can I say?

Peter and [stunt coordinator] Yuen Wo-Ping know the genre very well, so they didn't get in each other's way. They were a dream Hong Kong team. If scenes involved action, even the biggest, most expensive-looking shots—things had to go Mr. Yuen's way, because the shots had to work together. Peter had to work with that, and I can't think of a Hollywood cinematographer who would have that kind of patience. Because each shot had to be worked out, we were working in a sort of student-filmmaking or guerrilla-filmmaking style, but we had to make it great! We would sometimes set up the stunt or wire work only to find that the angle we wanted to use simply wouldn't work; we'd have to choose a new one, and Peter couldn't do his lighting until that was all set.

Peter was sometimes frustrated by our shooting style for the action scenes, because he wanted to make shots look so beautiful, but we didn't have those sequences planned in time for him to get the lighting exactly the way he wanted it. But for the dramatic scenes, Peter had the time he wanted, and he gave those shots a very artistic, refined look—it's very rich and classic, almost Hollywood in style. One of the tools that really helped us was the Power Pod crane arm. It gave us a lot of flexibility, and while it's generally used for very slow, smooth movements in Hollywood, the Hong Kong operators make it zoom everywhere, which is part of the genre's visual language.

AC: Most Hong Kong action films utilize a very contrasty lighting scheme and extremes in color temperature, but you went for a much more subdued look on this film.
Lee: Yes, we chose to recreate the look of classic Chinese watercolor paintings, so we used low-contrast film stock and also built that into the production design and lighting. It's semi-realistic, semi-abstract. But it is a Chinese aesthetic, and there's an old saying: "It's between like and unlike. Realism and fantasy." And that's where you want to be when you're trying to create art—realistic to bring people in emotionally, and fantastic to spark the imagination. To get there, we reduced the contrast in the film and used just the mid-tones. We took out blue for the most part, and we often went with a monotone palette, especially at night. It becomes more and more fantastic as the film goes on.

For me, the first half deals with the "crouching tiger, hidden dragon" in society—that is, people hidden beneath the surface of regulations and social codes. There is mystery, and things pop up unexpectedly. But later, that theme becomes more psychological and concerns hidden desires, so I thought it would feel right for the color to flatten out and become simpler. The fantasy aspect is more pronounced at night and later in the film.

AC: I'm surprised that you went with a 2.35:1 widescreen frame, because it seems that 1.85:1 would serve the fight scenes better by allowing you to get full body shots while remaining relatively close to the action.

Lee: I initially wanted to use a 1.66:1 or even 1.33:1 frame, because there is a lot of leaping action in the film and I thought the height of the frame would work well. We also have a lot of mountainous landscapes at the end of the film, so I was thinking of an Academy frame. Of course, at some theaters, especially in Asia, they would [not remove the 1.85 matte] in the projector and probably chop off a lot of heads! So then I thought about 1.85, until we did our location scout in the Gobi Desert; I knew we had to shoot those landscapes in widescreen. For a fight between two people, especially if they are using weapons, I think widescreen works well, but not for leaping action. Of course, you can do less up-and-down action and compose action that is more diagonal. You have to work within the frame, so we were at a disadvantage in some scenes.

Another decision was to shoot in the Super 35 format. Fred Elmes and I had used anamorphic on *Ride with the Devil*, which also had a lot of action, and while I thought that it was great for an epic look and for composition, the depth of field was much too shallow for what we needed on *Crouching Tiger*—[anamorphic] would have been too constricting on the performers. Anamorphic is a better tool for the widescreen look and composition, but not for this film. Of course, with Super 35, we did lose a bit of image quality with the blowup.

AC: What did you do differently in the desert scenes in terms of colors or compositions?

Lee: We used a lot of red to symbolize the passion between our two characters. This was the one portion of the film where the tiger and dragon were not hidden, though we reintroduced red at the end of the film in the cave scene to suggest that feelings were being revealed there as well. The desert also gave us a lot of yellows. However, there were a lot of questions about shooting those scenes at all, in that they [comprised] a very long flashback. In cinema language, the flashback has been out of date for forty years, but because this is a martial-arts fantasy film with a B-movie nature, I thought there was an excuse for doing it so bluntly. When we return to the present-day portion of the film, it's dominated by greens—suggesting the Jade Fox and the Green Destiny—and misty whites.

AC: How did you select Yuen Wo-Ping as your action coordinator?

Lee: Yuen Wo-Ping has been an idol of mine for many years. He's been directing films since I was in high school, and he even directed Jackie Chan's breakthrough films [1978's *Snake in the Eagle's Shadow* and 1979's *Drunken Master*]. He therefore has the experience; he's a better action director than I am, although I think I'm a better dramatic director! So it was a collaboration, an attempt to do something new with this film while keeping the flavor and raw energy of the genre, which he knows so well.

AC: Did he design his choreography with specific camera angles in mind?

Lee: Yes, but sometimes it's very obvious what has to be done, and I could design the shot myself. Peter would then go over [the scene] to make sure it didn't have any problems—that it didn't look too ugly—and then Mr. Yuen would have suggestions, maybe about the angle or the lens. His main concern was that his choreography looked its best. Peter is more like me, in that we wanted shots that worked best dramatically, thematically, or cinematically. So we would talk and compromise, with Peter and I usually deciding the shots.

AC: How much of the fighting action was undercranked to accentuate the speed?

Lee: Maybe half, but we never went under twenty frames per second. Almost every shot that is from the waist up is not undercranked. We used a lot of camera speeds to accentuate the action. We would also go as high as fifty fps to see exactly what was happening in some shots. With full-body shots, we'd go to twenty-two fps to add some energy, but we wouldn't go to twenty or twenty-one like they do on a lot of Hong Kong films; that looks jittery and funny.

The task of the fighting scenes in this film is not just to provoke excitement, but emotions as well. If they don't look real, that kills half the fun. For certain shots we used a digital crank-up in post if the action looked too slow. But unfortunately, the digital treatment looks like digital treatment! [*Laughs.*] There's no motion blur between frames, so the action jitters. It would probably be a very complex operation and very expensive to fix that problem, and we weren't in that budget league. We therefore tried not to use [that digital technique] too much, unless it was a very short portion of a shot for a specific effect. Otherwise, [we tried to] do everything in the camera.

AC: You describe the production as "guerrilla style," but didn't you have to design a lot of the coverage on the big stunt setups before shooting?
Lee: Peter would ask for story-boards on big setups, but we didn't have any. We tried to do as many rehearsals as possible, but by the time we'd get to the set, we just had to change everything. It's a question of not only what is workable and looks best, but also what the actors can do. While you may plan for one thing, you may have to do another. The shooting was very spontaneous, working from shot to shot, so Peter had to work very hard to make it look as if we'd planned it all!

AC: You describe *Crouching Tiger* as a boyhood dream come true. Were there images in your mind that you were able to finally realize with this picture?
Lee: Yes, like certain sequences that involve flying, and some of the fight scenes. One of the most difficult involved a chase scene in which the characters leap from rooftop to rooftop as the camera is flying over them, watching the action from above. Mr. Yuen is an expert in the style of wire work necessary for this kind of action, but one of the main reasons it had not been done before in Hong Kong films was the expense involved for the multiple cranes and platforms needed to "fly" the actors, and then the computer-effects work required to remove the wires.

Having the camera above the actors makes it impossible to hide the wires; you would generally do that by [shooting] up at the actor, whose body would then block the wires. There are a lot of cheesy techniques you can use to hide wires, like using smoke or smearing Vaseline on a part of the lens to blur it. But a lot of the ideas I had just weren't practical; there are reasons why people hadn't done some of the things I'd imagined, and I learned that the hard way.

AC: How did directing the action on *Crouching Tiger* compare to what you did on *Ride with the Devil*?
Lee: *Ride with the Devil* was essentially a Western, so it was very different. Still, it was good that I'd had that experience, because it taught me

to be aware of the danger involved in stunt work, the time-consuming nature of it, and how much preparation would be required. The martial-arts genre was another thing, however. It is very specific and demands its own technique, so I had a lot to learn from Mr. Yuen.

AC: Two things that are very different about martial-arts action are the physical intimacy and the speed of the action.
Lee: It's *very* quick. But I don't think that necessarily has to do with martial arts—it's about choreography, filmmaking, and the look.

AC: One of the things I've always enjoyed in Jackie Chan's films is the way he builds a dramatic story into the action scenes; there is a beginning, middle, and end.
Lee: You have to do that while writing the script, planning the choreography, and then [executing] the camerawork. It's boring to watch four solid minutes of fighting *bang bang bang bang.* Nobody can take watching that, but the stunt guys can keep at it for days! So there has to be a theme built into each fight scene to get the audience hooked, and each fight has to have a different style of coverage. The theme can be a specific kind of movement, storytelling, or just pure McGuffin, but you need a hook. You can also use different weapons and different rhythms in the choreography to break things up and make them more dramatic.

AC: Which other martial-arts films inspired you?
Lee: [*Laughs.*] All of them! I grew up with them and watched them all, even the boring ones. But I always enjoyed the earlier films, the Shaw Brothers films, Yuen Wo-Ping's films, and, of course, Bruce Lee's and Jackie Chan's films. The entire genre has inspired me, not necessarily specific films or filmmakers. But it's also not a very refined genre as a whole. They're generally popcorn movies, pure cinema.

AC: Can you describe the differences between shooting in mainland China and in the United States or England?
Lee: There's nobody else in the world like the Hollywood film crews. The main portion of our crew was from Hong Kong, so this was like making a Hong Kong film in China. The production support in China was very good, but everybody had to get used to the American style of filmmaking: the technology, size, efficiency, level of communication, organization, and the sophistication of the crew. Also, this was a drama and an action film—two movies in one—which made it very difficult to make

in China, because the story demanded a lot of company moves. We were centered in Beijing, where we had a lot of our locations and sets, but we traveled as far as the Summer Palace, which is a four-hour drive from the city, and the Gobi Desert in Xinjaing province, which took ten days of travel. Then we had another week's travel down to Zhejiang province in south China for the bamboo-forest sequences. It was a big production on a modest budget.

AC: I understand that with a budget of about $15 million, *Crouching Tiger, Hidden Dragon* was one of the biggest-budgeted films to ever shoot in China.

Lee: If I had actual money in my hands, it would be a little less, but budget-wise, compared to most Hong Kong films, this was like shooting *Titanic*. A big budget there is about $3 million, and that's why they don't spend a lot of time on dramas—they spend all of their money shooting the action scenes!

Ang Lee Tackles the Hulk

Paul Fischer / 2003

From *Film Monthly*, June 14, 2003. Reprinted by permission.

Oscar winner Ang Lee is one of Hollywood's most unique visionaries. The Taiwanese director has managed to take *Hulk* and transform it into his own personal vision while partially conforming to what Hollywood expects. It's a fine balancing act, but one he pulls off. He talked to Paul Fischer.

Paul Fischer: Will this movie be a challenge for the market?
Ang Lee: For the market or for me? I know it was for me.

PF: Do you think people will be surprised by this movie?
AL: Well, I think surprise is good, I don't really like "summer" movies myself and because it's a big movie it has to be released in summer, it is the only way they about launch it, summer or Christmas. There's a marketing side to it. As far as I'm concerned, it's my chance to do a big movie, it's a franchise. I don't need a big movie star to open big, it's a lot of money to make, that's ambitious, and so you have to sell it. To me I took advantage of the elements that are there, it can still be a filmmaker's vehicle and I grabbed the chance. It's like my new Hidden Dragon—you can mix the pulpy art which is a really guilty pleasure, it's hidden and you don't want to admit it, but it has a lot of juice in it and mix it with drama, which is always what I do and will probably always be what I do, with the human condition and psychology and I really like the back story. To me it's not a comic book super hero movie, it's a horror film.

PF: Was it hard to convince the studio not to go with a big-name actor, a superstar?
AL: No, it wasn't an issue at all because with the Hulk the CG actor is the

biggest star, he is more expensive than any star, so after that you have no money [laughs]. And they, like me, prefer brand new faces; it's more exciting. So it was no problem, I wanted Eric.

PF: So there was no question in your mind that you would make the Hulk CGI?

AL: I didn't know how to do that in the beginning. Larry Franco the line producer was the one, he showed me how *Jurassic Park* was done, and he had just come off *Jurassic Park 3*. Shot by shot, this was how it looks; this is how long it takes, the ways and means, how much it costs. He went through that shot by shot with me, and then we visited make-up companies, animatronics companies, and I got educated along the way, but it was pretty obvious that CGI was the best way to do it. From understanding what I wanted from the scene it had to be CGI.

PF: Were you a little anxious of working with the CGI?

AL: I didn't know enough to be frightened and then once I was frightened I was half way into it. ILM never said "no" to me; they said they could do it [laughs]. It's the producers and supervisors from our side that gave me the discipline. I found some things not satisfying, which is why I would jump in and do the Hulk myself [reference to pre-production videos where the director acted out how he wanted the Hulk to behave]. I didn't know how they used to do it, how they weren't directed or that animators would use their own faces looking in a mirror or a camera on themselves. And they are not performers. And often there's no reality in CGI characters, each time it looks like a different person so it has to be brought into some kind of continuity, starting with me performing it. It develops month by month, it's painstaking and a lot of craftsmanship, there's nothing fancy about it. It is frightening but when I got into it I didn't know it was like that.

PF: When did you first hear about the Hulk?

AL: I was promoting *Crouching Tiger*. It had just been released here and was getting very positive reviews and then big movies were offered to me. They felt I could bring something special, I guess if I can make a Chinese-language martial arts film which did that kind of business maybe I could do something with the genre. I think the Hong Kong style of filmmaking was particularly hip, and this particular project was found by James Schamus, my longtime collaborator.

PF: What was your initial reaction?

AL: First of all I didn't know what it was. Then I remembered the TV series with Lou Ferrigno painted in green and getting angry in slow motion. And then I checked out the Marvel Comics so it didn't take long before it clicked. So it's like my new Hidden Dragon, it's like a larger way of doing *Crouching Tiger* in America. I like the psychodrama, I like the hidden aggression, it's kind of Americana but universal. I like the subconscious having a physical manifestation and the layout of the backstory is very much of a psychodrama.

PF: Did you read all the comics?

AL: Oh, a lot. Started with the Thesis, the Essential, and then I kept all the favorite parts near me.

PF: But this is very much an Ang Lee film as opposed to a more typical summer blockbuster?

AL: Oh yes. There was no doubt about that. I just had to prove that I could pull it off.

PF: Do you get involved in the marketing side of the film?

AL: No, that's not my department. It's a brand new experience. I don't want to partake in that. I'd go to the marketing meetings like twice, it's immense. But I told them that I wanted to draw the line. I just make the movie—that's all I care about. I sell it the way I'm used to, talking to journalists and that's all I can do. I don't want to talk on the video game, I don't want to do anything to do with the merchandise. It's great they have to do that to sell a big summer movie, but I've no knowledge and don't know how to go about it.

PF: Do you see these kinds of stories as modern-day myths?

AL: I see it as modern-day myth. I took a lot from horror films, Frankenstein, King Kong, things like that, Jekyll and Hyde and a lot of Greek mythology and pseudo-science, all sorts. It's kind of lowbrow art, it's very juicy, it's not delicate but it's definitely juicy—it depends what you make out of it.

PF: There are some very obviously comic book–styled visuals with the split screens you use at certain points. How much of that do you storyboard?

AL: It's all in the editing room. I start out wanting to do it. This is one of the reasons I found an excuse to do something I always wanted to do. Why do we always line them up in a linear way? Why can't we do like martial arts choreography? Choreograph images, having images like a comic book when you open a page, go to the most prominent design structure and it has a cause, your eyes go different places, they pick and choose, back and forth and it was "how can we do that in a movie?" to a certain extent. So I was always thinking about doing that, and we explored those possibilities but by the time we were shooting we didn't know what we were doing [laughs]. And the cinematographer was reluctant to give in to that because they want to expose as much as they can to get the best quality. If you leave some room for potential split screen, maybe you don't use it and then a scene will look bad; you will have to crop it and it looks really bad. So at the end of the day, I just shot the hell out of it with lots of cameras, every possibility, which is a headache for the sound guy because you might end up using a close-up where his mike is right up there. It's very frustrating and you find out why people don't do that in the first place. But then in the editing room little by little it started to happen.

PF: What was it about Eric Bana that you liked so much for this role?
AL: I figured in the comic books nobody wanted to see Bruce Banner, they just wanted to see the Hulk come out. The guy is a loser, a wimp. But by simplified drawing you are able to project your own melancholy into him. But a movie is different. I was hoping to get something and have that melancholic demeanor and of course I always go for a good actor, which Eric is, and someone who could be sympathetic. I saw him in an Australian movie, *Chopper*, and that was Hulk for me. And Ridley Scott was kind enough to show me an early cut of *Black Hawk Down* and his scenes in that. In *Black Hawk Down* people complain they couldn't tell who is who, but I think you remember Eric. He was my choice and the studio really like him.

PF: Will you do *Hulk 2*?
AL: I have no idea. It's in development but I'm so drained by the first one, I have no thoughts about the second one.

PF: But you've made a period costume drama, a film set in the American Civil War, and a martial arts film. What would you like to do next?

AL: I don't know. I would like to do something different. I live in New York with my wife and two boys and I will go home. I'm in the process of de-Hulking right now! [laughs] It's kind of painful, the adrenalin slows down, but I'm not thinking about the future yet.

PF: Is it true that you felt sick when you saw trees because they are green?
AL: I did get a little sick of the color green [laughs]. He is a CG character—what am I supposed to do. But yeah for a long time I was really sick of the color green.

PF: Will we get more CGI actors in the future?
AL: It's a lot cheaper to use real actors, believe me, even big stars. A lot easier and a lot cheaper, if you can get them to say the lines, it's a lot easier with real actors.

PF: What was your childhood like back in Taiwan?
AL: Repressed I guess. Not much fun. That's why I've had a midlife crisis—I was looking for fun. My father was the principal of the high school, the best one in Taiwan, and he was my principal. And I was a very shy, docile kind of kid, I didn't go out or anything, I was very quiet . . . private tutors, go to school, study, sitting there all the time but my mind wasn't in a book, and it was somewhere else.

PF: One of the themes of the film is genetic engineering. What are your thoughts on that?
AL: We are at the point where we are facing a lot of fundamental questions about who we are, I think. I think we are at a crucial point. There's always been a fear of science, ever since the industrial revolution. I think Frankenstein is an early example of that. We are afraid that we will build something that will turn on us, something that is out of control. Dramatically it interests me because the artificial brings out the innocence and the aggression, the real you, it has a physical manifestation and that's interesting. I'm not a scientist but we are now into genetic engineering to improve ourselves, to stretch ourselves—that's a big question, about who we are. Is that you or a little machine? I guess the only sense of yourself is memories and that's why the movie deals with memory a lot. With the collective memory of human beings. I think we face a lot of metaphysical and fundamental questions about who we are.

PF: Do you believe in God?

AL: I'm pretty much a student of the Chinese philosophies and we don't really talk about it, anything three feet above your head you have to show respect and not pretend you know or imagine that somebody like you that created it. We just don't talk about it. I put a lot in the movie actually. Big things, small things, there are just off balance with something. The big mushroom cloud caused by a bunch of atoms.

PF: Were you surprised by Nick Nolte's passion for science and his knowledge?

AL: Yeah, totally. I just envision him doing it. And because he is a respected actor who for ten, twelve years has turned away from Hollywood, he only wants to do small films, he had enough. And I had to go there and show respect and give him the pitch. I went to his house in Hollywood and it was the most gothic experience I ever had. It was this weird collection of stuff from all around the world. And I was sitting by the fireplace and after five minutes he said "you must come up and see my blood." And I went upstairs and there was a lab with hundreds of bottles of something and there's an electronic monitor. So he pricks his own finger and watches on this monitor his own [blood] cells and he went through that and I said something like, can you make it colorful and he was impressed and we went downstairs and talked some more about science. So he was the role. He said "oh I'm on my down time in between films, I can get in shape." I had to bite my tongue because I just wanted to say "oh no, just come as you are. . . ." He knew the Hulk but he didn't know what role. I was talking about Greek tragedy and he was into it.

PF: You spent a lot of time exacting things for how the Hulk should be. How did that come about?

AL: It was out of necessity and desperation. I wanted to show them. Maybe there was a bit of my childhood, things I never fulfilled, coming out, too. I was just about the most spaced-out child you could ever meet; people always tell me I am the most spaced-out person they have ever met in their lives. I was like absentminded. I couldn't help it because I had an attention span problem and I would be talking or reading and I would be somewhere else.

PF: You started as an actor—why did you switch?

AL: I couldn't speak English, that's why. I came to the States and I couldn't get into the actor's program. It was very frustrating to me. It was a three-year program and they were the elite and then I didn't really want to be on stage because I couldn't really make it as an actor, and I thought if I had to direct, I wanted to be a movie director, that's my performance. I always thought movies were my way of performing. After a long while I began to get comfortable behind the camera as a watcher, rather than being watched; gradually, over a long period of time, I switched positions. Until lately when the *Hulk* started to come out.

PF: Eric Bana said you were a philosophical director. What's your take on that?

AL: I don't know, maybe that's their take on me. It's a way to encourage them I guess, something abstract and then you nail them down in the actual act so they feel they are creating something interesting. I guess I like to do philosophical thoughts, but in making movies you can only do so much and then you have to throw it away and see how it plays; you have to level with everybody, otherwise a concept is dead and philosophy can be pretentious. Sometimes I hate it's called a film—I like the old name, movie. Like people are here, you move them to there. It's a movie.

PF: Do you want to make a small movie?

AL: Yeah. But when I make it now it will be more expensive now. People charge me more. There will be a lot more people aware of it. But yeah I would like different challenges, I would like the freedom not bound by budget, big or small. I do like to make a small movie sometime.

PF: Is Hitchcock an influence?

AL: Yeah I love him. He is one of my heroes that has done all the weird stuff disguised in popular films, and he did it so well and I do admire him, although when I do the same thing I have to update it. Similar take on Freud and stuff can look too simple today. I like to have a different angle. But yeah, he is my hero.

Paul Fischer is originally from Australia. Now he is an interviewer and film critic living in Hollywood.

Ride the High Country

Peter Bowen / 2005

From *Filmmaker* 14, no. 1 (October 2005): 34–39. Reprinted by permission.

When news broke that Ang Lee's new movie, *Brokeback Mountain*, was about gay cowboys, some salacious wags giggled, dubbing it "Homo on the Range" and "Bareback Mountain." But after it screened at this year's Venice Film Festival, where it won the Golden Lion, the laughter stopped. And, for most of the audience, it was replaced by tears. The movie—due out this winter from Focus Features—is a heartbreaking saga of two men in love set against the backdrop of America's contemporary West, and it demonstrates again Lee's talent for staging complex human dramas that are both deeply conventional *and* culturally radical.

The original story by E. Annie Proulx was published in the *New Yorker* in 1997, where Larry McMurtry and Diana Ossana read it and were inspired to adapt it to the screen. For the next seven years, the project kicked around Hollywood—it was at one time attached to Joel Schumacher and at another to Gus Van Sant—where it gathered dust as well as admiration as one of the great unproduced screenplays. Eventually, Lee, coming off the exhaustion of having done two complicated action pictures, remembered it and got producer James Schamus and Focus Features, which Schamus is co-president of, on board.

The story, at once intimate and epic, follows two cowboys—Ennis Del Mar (Heath Ledger) and Jack Twist (Jake Gyllenhaal)—who meet during the summer of 1963 herding sheep up on Brokeback Mountain. Buoyed by the mountain's beauty and sheltered by its privacy, the two men find that something is unleashed between them that neither can explain nor let go of. Off the mountain they go their separate ways. Twist bounces about Texas as a second-rate rodeo cowboy before marrying Lureen (Anne Hathaway), the daughter of a well-to-do farm machinery retailer. Del Mar stays in Wyoming, gets hitched to his sweetheart, Alma

65

(Michelle Williams), and tries to settle down to being a ranch hand and father. That is, until Twist sends him a postcard and the dam of emotions that has been building up since that summer on Brokeback Mountain breaks wide open.

The ensuing romance takes place over a twenty-year period, during which the great changes occurring in America barely register a ripple in this western backcountry. But as the characters age, the story itself changes. What begins as a virile, boot-slapping paean to the American western and its not-so-subtle homoeroticism slowly evolves into a meditation on love, longing, and regret. Lee, with the help of production designer Judy Becker and d.p. Rodrigo Prieto, has envisioned a West split in two. High up on Brokeback is the American dream; below, in the rusty rural towns, is America's waking reality. It's a division that the last election made painfully clear.

Peter Bowen: This is the second film—*The Wedding Banquet* being the first—which focuses on gay men. What is it about them that interests you?

Ang Lee: I grew up believing in the Chinese idea in Taiwan, believing in education, the nationalist party, my parents and all that. When I found a lot of that was phony, it sort of turned me upside down. I think that experience when I was twenty-three and I first came to the States, no longer believing in the place I came from, but also not being an American, made me realize that I have and will all my life be a foreigner, an outsider. That makes it very easy for me to see the world, the straight world, from a different angle. In my films, I always identify with the outsider, like the characters of Tobey [Maguire] and Jeffrey [Wright] in *Ride with the Devil*. Also, I understand things not being as we were told they were. That America, the Civil War, the seventies are not as we were told. So if I see material that looks very real to me and has a different angle and it is not what we see in public or in the media, then I find that very interesting.

PB: From the storytelling point of view, is it interesting to have characters who innately have secrets?

AL: Yes, and some sort of confusion. Probably in the city now, gay men don't have confusion, but in the setting of the story, the two men, especially Ennis, have no vocabulary, no understanding, of what they are experiencing. And when Ennis finally does understand, it is too late. He has missed it. That makes the story really poignant. To me that is also a universal feeling—that we have missed something.

PB: Which is also the plot of the classic love story, nostalgia for the moment that has past, that moment when you fell in love.
AL: For me, it is the nature of the true western, and not so much the movie-genre, gunslinger-type of western. A lot of westerns and western literature are really about the West disappearing, and that gives them a sort of elegiac feeling.

PB: Many critics have argued that the western as a genre appeared at the very moment that the actual West, or what we think of as the Wild West, disappeared. But this is a movie about the contemporary West. How did the project get started?
AL: James [Schamus] sent me the story as something that was floating around as a movie project. That was during the Good Machine [a production company] days. He thought it was something special but wasn't sure if it was doable. I read the short story, and I choked up at the end. It was so special that I almost didn't really know that language. It was almost more pure and special than the westerns I'd seen. Of course, a lot of the goodness of the material comes from Annie Proulx's writing, a lot of the inner depictions that are hard to put onscreen. I then read Larry Mc-Murtry and Diana Ossana's script, which made it work. It is extremely loyal to the short story.

PB: But you didn't make it right away. What happened?
AL: *Hulk.* I was already signed up to do that, and I also heard some other directors had signed on to make *Brokeback*. After Hulk, after two really long movies, I was wrecked. I was going to take a break, but then I got depressed that I was taking a break. So I asked James, "Remember that *Brokeback* project? That is one story that sticks in my head. What happened to it? Did it turn out to be a good movie?" And he told me it hadn't been done. Then the thing started crawling back into me. I knew that I should be doing that film, that if I didn't do it, I would really regret it. When I do a movie there is always that feeling, that the script belongs to me, or rather that I belong to it. It will use me and consume me.

PB: You obviously connected to the story. Did you also have any association with the landscape in which the story takes place?
AL: Only as a tourist. *Ride with the Devil* was sort of a pre-western. Only the last shot was on the verge of that landscape. And I found the desert romantic, especially after doing *Crouching Tiger* and *Hulk*. But I wasn't connected to that western landscape of high mountains and such.

When I read the short story, and even the script, there was no picture of the landscape in my head. It was all about gay ranch hands; how they go about their emotions and how poignant it was.

PB: Your movie is so much about the landscape. When did that vision set in?

AL: It is usually when I do location scouting that I start to fashion the look and the pace of the movie in my head. I did location scouting in two areas. I went to Wyoming twice, one time getting the tour from Annie Proulx herself, and the other area was suggested by Larry McMurtry, and that was more along the west of Wyoming. The two had different ideas about where Brokeback is—her idea was Big Horn Mountain, and that is where I went first. McMurtry thought it was further west. In the end I had to make the film in Canada, so I had to find a similar essence based on my memory of Wyoming.

PB: What was the reason for going to Canada?

AL: Several reasons. It was financial in terms of tax breaks and unions. And because there was no filmmaking in Wyoming, we would have had to bring everyone there.

PB: Talk about casting. Were Heath Ledger and Jake Gyllenhaal your first choices?

AL: Actually I had someone else in mind when I read the story. But after I realized the importance of the time lapses in the film, I decided to go with younger actors.

PB: Because it is easier to make someone older, rather than younger?

AL: Yes. I cast Heath first—he was a very natural Ennis—and then I cast Jake, because I really like him. But I was a little worried that he wouldn't be "cowboy enough," not rural enough.

PB: Gyllenhaal reminded me a lot of Montgomery Clift in Howard Hawks's *Red River*. A sort of pretty cowboy.

AL: He also has that knowing look, and the way he looks up with such yearning—Clift had the same feel in *The Misfits*.

PB: Another modern-day story told in the West . . .

AL: . . . that is also about the loss of the West.

PB: This film also marks a brand new crew—d.p., production designer, editor—for you.

AL: After *Hulk* I was wrecked, so I told myself, if I want to do this, I need to start with everyone new to help me forget about the past. I felt bad about my old crew. They sort of understand, but I don't think they really understand why I had to go through that. You work with the right chemistry of people, and it lasts for a while, but then you need something new to refresh yourself. It is healthy to do as an artist, but as a friend it hurts sometimes.

PB: It must have been tough not to have the same vocabulary and short-hand you have with people you work with a lot. How did you work with d.p. Rodrigo Prieto to create the film's look?

AL: He had never done anything like this before. His strength was in Mexican movies—gritty, handheld, that sort of thing. I explained that we needed a serene quality, which is sort of the opposite of what he had traditionally been hired to do.

PB: Were there westerns, like Anthony Mann's big country epics, that inspired the look?

AL: I used photography and painting much more than I used western movies. One normally thinks of Ansel Adams in terms of the American West, but I didn't really want to do that. I looked at others, like Richard Avedon's *Photographs of the American West*. And I looked at a lot of contemporary photographs of small towns. They used high contrast, with a wacky frame and lots of low shadows. I took a lot of inspiration from those photos. And I noticed that they put a lot of emphasis on the sky; they tilt up quite a bit.

PB: And for paintings?

AL: Mostly classic western paintings, like from the Hudson River School. I looked at [nineteenth-century landscape painter] Martin Heade when it came to clouds and contrast. His work shows a very soft, not harsh, contrast. I also used Edward Hopper for the diner scene, and for that one scene where Heath meets Jake's parents, I looked at Andrew Wyeth.

PB: You make a stylistic contrast between the mountains and their small towns. What kind of dramatic or symbolic distinction did you want to make?

AL: The mountains were magic, and everyday life sucks! As for the changes in the story, I told Judy Becker that we are doing a period piece in a timeless place. When we called upon a thousand extras in Canada to play a rodeo scene in Wyoming, we didn't have to change a thing, because not much changes there.

PB: What about costume and makeup? How did you work on aging the characters?
AL: For the women, we couldn't really put on lines, so the hair becomes really all you can do. Each time she shows up she has a different hairdo and different hair color.

PB: The film is oddly conventional and radical. How are audiences treating it?
AL: It is tricky. So far, the audience is fairly sophisticated. When I set out to do this, I thought, this will be strictly arthouse because of the subject matter and the way it was in my head. The very early screenings just told me what to tweak. I remember James told me, "Right now it's three hankies and two bladders, and the goal is four hankies and one bladder."

PB: All bodily fluids.
AL: At the first public screening in Venice, I was surprised. The feeling was a lot warmer than I expected. Going in, they were calling it a gay cowboy [story], and then they stopped and started just calling it a love story. One pretty conservative person found it disturbing because he didn't feel that there was anything wrong when he saw the tent scene. It makes me a little nervous when I think that it will go wider than arthouse. I asked James in the marketing meeting if we could just release it in the blue states, and everybody cracked up.

Firestorm

Rebecca Davies / 2008

From *New Statesman* 137, no. 4878 (2008): 34–36. Reprinted by permission

Ang Lee's work has often been described as cold. The muted, lonesome prairies of *Brokeback Mountain* (2005), the frozen woodlands and dislocated relationships of *The Ice Storm* (1997), the stylization that keeps characters apart in *Crouching Tiger, Hidden Dragon* (2000) and even the stifling social conventions in *Sense and Sensibility* (1995) have all served to perpetuate this chilly reputation. And yet the little man in the cozy grey jumper who is perched on the sofa opposite me is anything but cold. He is warm, humble, charming and, above all, intensely passionate about making films.

That passion—in both the physical and the emotional sense—is something he has had to draw on in abundance for his latest feature, *Lust, Caution*. Lee's first Chinese-language film since *Crouching Tiger, Hidden Dragon*, it is based on a short story by the acclaimed novelist Eileen Chang and is set in Hong Kong and Japanese-occupied Shanghai during the Second World War. It tells the story of a young woman who uses her talent as an actress to seduce the head of the secret service, who is collaborating with the Japanese, with the intention of luring him to his death at the hands of the resistance. In doing so, she initiates a sadomasochistic game of cat and mouse in which the roles are constantly reversing and nothing, not even her own identity, is certain.

The only place where all pretense is shed is in the bedroom, where three long, graphic, and often violent sex scenes play out. It took twelve days to film these exhausting and disturbing episodes, and they have gained the film an NC-17 rating in the United States. This is a huge blow to *Lust, Caution*'s distribution because, given the pornographic stigma that still clings to an NC-17 rating, many cinemas simply will not show the film. But Lee has refused to edit out the sex scenes for US audiences, insisting that they are absolutely essential to a full understanding of the work.

"The whole of the second half of the film is charted by those three sex scenes. I shot them early on in the schedule so they would help me craft everything that comes after. The precise angles of the body help to visualize the characters' emotions and how they relate to one another in the film as a whole, as well as providing guidance to the audience. But thanks to the rating, it will be hard to drag people in to a movie that is seen as the cultural equivalent of a porn film."

The aggressive and demeaning way in which the female lead (played by newcomer Tang Wei) is treated in the film has raised comparisons between *Lust, Caution* and Bernardo Bertolucci's *Last Tango in Paris*, in which Maria Schneider is subjugated sexually by a far older Marlon Brando. But Lee denies that his film is misogynistic. "The story is written by a woman from a woman's point of view, and Wong Chia Chi [Tang Wei] is a strong character. I think this provides a fresh angle on female sexuality, especially when contrasted with the political aspect, which is usually very patriarchal. The woman's perspective is like the dark side of the moon: it always exists, but it is never exposed, at least not in my culture."

In the course of the film, Tang Wei's character evolves from naive, or-phaned schoolgirl to ambivalent femme fatale under the alias of Mrs. Mak. A former Miss Universe finalist, Tang is fairly well known from her work for Chinese stage and television, but had no film experience whatever prior to this. So how did Lee manage to coax such a convincing—and demanding—performance from her? "When I cast her, I couldn't think about whether she was strong enough to take it or not; I just had to believe in her, and hope that belief would become the strength. As long as she wasn't crushed by the work, we just kept building on her character day by day. If she started to get too comfortable with the routine and the abusive nature of my directing, we would have to give an extra dosage of pressure at the end of the week, because she had to be stimulated to make her change and evolve."

It is hard to imagine someone so affable being "abusive." Lee laughs. "It's only abusive on the surface. And anyway, the toughness is mutual. The actors want it as much as I want it. It's not about pleasing me; it's about whether they hit the standard I set or not. And in the case of Tang Wei, I chose her from ten thousand other actresses because I felt she was a lot like me."

According to Lee, it is his identification with, and respect for women that allow him to place them in such grueling situations. "In my culture, there's a tradition that when you're in an overwhelming situation and you don't know what to do, you put yourself in a woman's shoes. I guess this makes it easier for me in a dramatic situation to identify more with women than with men. I'm not macho. I'm not a Mel Gibson sort of person." In fact, Lee has first-hand experience of what it's like to fulfill the woman's conventional role. After failing, much to the disappointment of his teacher father, to get into university in his native Taiwan, he went to drama school in Taiwan and then completed a master's degree in film production at New York University, but then remained unemployed for six years. His wife, the microbiologist Janice Lin, was the sole breadwinner for them both and their two sons while he worked as a full-time house husband.

Lee finally got his film breakthrough when he won first and second places in a screenwriting competition organized by the Taiwanese government in 1990. But his biggest break was being asked to direct Emma Thompson's screen adaptation of Jane Austen's *Sense and Sensibility*. This won him his second Golden Bear, as well as bagging seven Academy Award nominations in its own right. Following a dip in commercial success with his next two films—*The Ice Storm* and *Ride with the Devil*—he once again grabbed the world's attention with *Crouching Tiger, Hidden Dragon*, his revival of the martial-arts epic as a genre, which notched up Oscar nominations for Best Picture and Best Director, and won the prize for Best Foreign-Language Film. But then in 2003 came Lee's part-CGI comic-book adaptation *Hulk*, a box-office flop that polarized critics and left most audiences baffled and alienated.

Physically and mentally drained, his confidence knocked, Lee considered early retirement, he now admits. Encouragement came from an unlikely source: his father, who had hitherto expressed little more than dismay at his son's chosen career path. "If it was a choice between making movies and doing nothing, he'd probably still wish me to make movies," laughs Lee. "So he made me keep going."

It was fortunate he did; Lee's next film was *Brokeback Mountain*, the "gay western" that won the hearts of audiences worldwide, as well as a Best Director Oscar for Lee. "After *Hulk* I was exhausted and felt unhealthy, but then *Brokeback* really brought me back to life and to love of filmmaking. I didn't know it was going to be a big success. I thought that people wouldn't pay it much attention. I just wanted to enjoy making that movie because I loved the material so much."

So what next for a man who has covered every genre from period drama to cartoons and cowboy films? Despite rumors on the Internet that he has agreed to direct *A Little Game*, an adaptation of a play by Jean Dell that's the latest project of his long-time collaborator James Schamus, Lee insists he has no plans.

"I have to feel passionate enough about a project before I agree to come on board. But it will most likely be another adaptation." It seems odd that someone with a well-demonstrated gift for screenwriting should be so eager to use other people's material. "I'm quite lazy," the director explains." I prefer to find a ready-written piece of literature that's already great, and I snatch the idea. I find the writing process very lonely, very painful. I only started out writing because, at a young age, nobody would give me anything to work with. I was just earning my right to direct." *Lust, Caution* is a masterful evocation of one of the uneasiest periods in China's history, as distilled in the power struggle between one couple.

The measured pacing ensures that every scene, whether depicting the mundane or the melodramatic, is charged with fear and suspense, eliciting subtle yet insightful performances from the actors. Yet Lee fears his efforts will not be recognized at this year's Oscars because of the film's limited distribution and because *Lust, Caution* has been withdrawn as Taiwan's entry for Best Foreign-Language Film. According to the Academy of Motion Picture Arts and Sciences, "an insufficient number of Taiwanese participated in the production of the film" for it to qualify.

But Lee says he is more concerned that people understand and respond to his film's message than he is with personal accolades. "I want *Lust, Caution* to provoke closer examination of ourselves—not only our sexual desire or our motivations, but how we see the world. That's 'lust,' in Chinese. It doesn't mean just love or sex, but anything with color, a phenomenon that you see as reality, including emotion that you think is real, a reflection of the truth.

"Not that I provide any answers. But it's an invitation to take a look at ourselves, our rationalities, so we can peel them off to see the subconscious beneath. Everyone has their own particular lust, but let's take a look and see what that is." *Lust, Caution* is out now on general release.

Cruel Intentions

Nick James / 2008

From *Sight and Sound* 18, no. 1 (January 2008): 47–50. Reprinted by permission.

The latest film by Ang Lee—*Lust, Caution*—encases its tale of a society in which nothing is as it seems in a glittering carapace of athletic eroticism and the glamour of Hong Kong and Shanghai in the late 1930s. Nick James talks to the director about how the film answered to his midlife crisis.

Ang Lee is talking pleasantries and holding the palm of his right hand flat against his cheek. I'm concerned he may be in pain (dental? hangover?), but with interview time ticking by I say nothing. It's a milky-grey Monday morning at the Soho Hotel in London. The first weekend of the Times BFI 51st London Film Festival has perhaps taken its toll. Ang Lee's superb new film *Lust, Caution* (*Se, jie*) has just had its gala premiere to much acclaim and some surprise at the realistic erotic scenes between the leads Tony Leung and Tang Wei.

These slightly exhausted interview circumstances could not be further from the mood of *Lust, Caution*, which captures the bright, energized surfaces of a life lived in fakery, in the superficially glamorous but highly dangerous cities of Hong Kong and Shanghai from 1938 to 1942. Newcomer Tang Wei plays Wang Chia Chi, a Shanghai-born student turned actress in Hong Kong. She's the featured lead in propaganda plays aimed at rousing Chinese patriotism against the Japanese invaders of the mainland. When elements of the collaborationist party led by Wang Jingwei, beholden and sympathetic to the Japanese, arrive in the city, the theatre troupe's leader Kuang Yu Min (Wang Leehom—a popstar in Asia) recruits Wong Chia Chi to his nascent guerrilla group. Kuang wants the group to assassinate Mr. Yee (Tony Leung), one of Wang Jingwei's ministers. Wong Chia Chi must use her acting skills to lure Mr. Yee to his death by pretending to be a disillusioned married woman and becoming his lover. For the ruse to work, she must first lose her virginity to the only boy among the group with experience, a boorish fellow who visits prostitutes.

We learn all this and much more in flashback from the film's opening moment in 1942 Shanghai, when a sophisticated and worldly Wong Chia Chi, now transformed into Mrs. Mak, is about to betray Mr. Yee at last. Before the film's finale, which returns to that opening moment, we will see Mrs. Mak sit at Mrs. Yee's Mahjong table and engage in social chitchat that barely masks a vicious politesse born of unequal social standing; we will see the original attempt to entrap Mr. Yee end in bloody chaos; and we will see Wong Chia Chi engage in passionate, anatomically realistic and varied acts of sexual congress with her seemingly cruel lover.

The film is based on a short story by Eileen Chang, and like its predecessor in Ang Lee's canon, *Brokeback Mountain* (2005), its subtle and heartbreaking pleasures are to be found in the way cinema has expanded a piece of literature rather than the usual pattern of contraction that novel adaptations entail. Both films are arguably about what we hide about ourselves and how that contorts our lives, yet the new movie seems more interested in the maintenance of coldness against the pressure of passion, whereas *Brokeback* focused on finding relief from the requirements to be unfeeling. If *Lust, Caution* seems a little emotionally cooler than *Brokeback*, that's an endemic aspect of the espionage genre, and in this case only adds to the quietly devastating effect of the melodrama.

When the interview that follows is over, I ask Ang Lee about his jaw. He says there's nothing wrong: it's just a gesture he picked up while making *Lust, Caution*. I hope he's not pretending.

Nick James: Was the Oscar hullabaloo around *Brokeback Mountain* one of the reasons why you chose a Chinese subject and production for your next project?

Ang Lee: That's not totally why I wanted to do *Lust, Caution*—in fact, I was working on the script during the *Brokeback* campaign. Thinking back, the two films are almost like sister works. At the age of forty-five, I started to have a midlife crisis because of the way I was living out my childhood fantasy. So I got into subject matter I'd never paid attention to before, namely romance. Both films are based on stories that are not much more than thirty pages long, both tales of impossible romance written by gutsy women. So while it's true that I didn't feel like doing another American film after *Brokeback*, that was not the main reason.

NJ: What does Eileen Chang's work mean to your Chinese audience?

AL: She's probably the most beloved author in modern Chinese litera-ture and most people have read a lot of her work. Her most famous sto-ries were written in the early 1940s, before she was twenty-five. She was banned in China for many years but much of her writing has been avail-able for the last decade or so.

Lust, Caution is a story hardly anybody had read, including myself. I discovered it maybe three years ago and it made me wonder, is this really Eileen Chang? She usually writes big, revered works as if from an oracle, but this short story has none of that feeling. It's written very concisely and sparely, almost like an old film noir, very strange and so cruel it's almost unbearable.

This is the only one of her stories that's about herself, about what killed love for her. She fell for and married a collaborator of the Japa-nese invaders, a high official in Wang Jingwei's puppet government, who dumped her after two years. That's what she's writing about: she's comparing female sexuality with the war against the Japanese. She spent years covering it up, rewriting and rewriting, and the story wasn't pub-lished until twenty-five years after she first drafted it. I was attracted to it not because I wanted to adapt Eileen Chang but because "Lust, Caution" is so different from her other work. Her more typical books have been made into movies many times—though none of them, in my opinion, is successful because they all revere the writing too much.

NJ: So did you change a lot?

AL: In spirit, no. I just expanded it, tried to figure out the gaps. The two obvious changes were suggested by my co-writer/producer James Scha-mus—no Chinese person would have initiated either of them. One is the moment when Wong Chia Chi's group is exposed in Hong Kong just after Mr. Yee has eluded them, and the boys have to kill the traitor. This not only introduces action to the midpoint of the movie and separates the two halves, which I treat as two different films, but it also acts like a rite of passage for the boys, their equivalent of Wong Chia Chi having to lose her virginity in order to play the unfaithful wife of a businessman. James's other idea was to go to the jewelry shop where the film's climax occurs twice, to set it up. And of course there's an extension of the sex scenes: Eileen Chang suggested them but she didn't go into the details.

NJ: We've never seen anything as explicit from you before. Does that also come out of your midlife crisis?

AL: It's more a post-midlife crisis. My real crisis was during the five years of making *Crouching Tiger, Hidden Dragon* (2000) and *The Hulk* (2003). Throughout *The Hulk* I was sort of collapsed: I finally had to admit I'm not that young anymore, and lust was one of the things I had to face up to by not being too repressed or shy to deal with it.

After a midlife crisis you have to choose what's most important. And facing it was like hell. It went against my superficial nature to deal with deeper, subconscious desires, though I think it was very valuable, very eastern in a way. The psychology of sex comes from a western approach, but "lust" in Chinese means not just lust for sex but lust for life and also color. It's a projection of your own desire, of your own point of view, your motivation. But you have to be careful, because any passion—sex, or a lust for being good, such as patriotism—will make fools of us. Caution, however, is rational. So the title *Lust, Caution* is in the same realm as *Sense and Sensibility*—and *Se, jie* is also the symbol of the ring, the diamond ring, the boundaries of love.

NJ: There's a beautiful little book by Donald Richie that explains Japanese aesthetics. I wish there was an equivalent for the Chinese.

AL: There's a huge difference between people who use phonetics for language transcription and those who use characters, as in China. The Chinese system is more like movies, like montage, like drawing with sight and sound. The shape itself means something, so when you see the word it resonates in your head. When the Chinese see *Lust, Caution* in characters with the comma in between it has a shocking vibe.

NJ: The film seems to depict a surface that barely conceals what's going on, so the texture has to be simultaneously superficial and deep.

AL: Cinema has certain forms you have to borrow from, and one of these is genre. I looked at film noir but instead of a lot of shadow I used depth of focus and color, trying to find a new way to do it. The other genre I drew on was the patriotic melodramas I grew up with. The old-fashioned, romantic films noirs in which you are lost in the mystery—films like *Laura* (1944) or *Notorious* (1946)—have elements of both. And the characters in *Lust, Caution* emulate that: whether in staging a patriotic play that gets people really worked up or when Wong Chia Chi goes to see Cary Grant and Ingrid Bergman to pick up their attitude and copy them. I prefer the romantic, over-the-top noirs to the films of the later

1940s, after Hitchcock, which get meaner and meaner and lose that lavish emotion.

NJ: There are also aspects of the espionage movie.

AL: There's a mix. There's a level of playing, which is lust—including sex—and then there's psychology underneath. And the Mahjong scenes are like a war movie played out on a Mahjong table. But when people say it's an espionage thriller it makes me nervous. The plot isn't as tight as it should be for pure espionage and all the psychology means everything is prolonged. So if you tell a British audience *Lust, Caution* belongs to the espionage genre you might arouse expectations that the film doesn't fulfill.

NJ: For the Chinese this period was a time of atrocity and destruction, but for the West it's imbued with exotic appeal. The film looks beautiful and seductive and you *seem* to play those two ideas against each other.

AL: For the West Shanghai was sin city, an eastern Casablanca. So I did have that sense. And inevitably when you put *qipao* [cheongsams] inside the film, the modern style of *qipao*—shorter, with short sleeves—and then you put a western hat on her and a trenchcoat over her, it's got to be exotic, even for the Chinese. With *qipao* you have to walk in small steps and in a trenchcoat you want to swagger, so how do you manage that combination? But I didn't play that up fully because I didn't want the style to take over.

NJ: I get the sense that your decision-making was affected by your nervousness about the drift of the film's direction.

AL: That's *often* been the case for me. If I'm doing a standard genre film, I always think there are people who know the form better—not least my producer and some of the audience. And then the film begins to seem like a work I have to deliver, it makes me feel like a craftsman. There's nothing wrong with that—you can produce great art from craftsmanship and I'm an avid film learner: I feel I want to be forever a film student, that people are paying me to learn how to make movies. But if I touch a certain genre then I have to exercise it further otherwise I feel uneasy—not only am I not doing my best, but I'm conforming somehow.

NJ: You are working again with your long-term producer-writer partner James Schamus on a Chinese subject. Is this a leap for him?

AL: Whenever we do a Chinese project there's a stage where I wish I could get away from him [laughs]. At some point he'll want to read the script because he'll be the producer and he's the best distributor for my film. And then through translation, or the loss in translation, he'll get a bite of it and he'll have his criticisms. Some I can overcome, some I can't. So he'll have his input. And the best way to give input is to write it into the script instead of sixty pages of notes.

There's something in Chinese film culture that accommodates what I want to do—and then James comes to help. Cinema, after all, is a culture established by westerners, mostly Americans, and they *are* just better at some things: structure and also certain mannerisms I borrow from genres and don't know enough about. That stuff comes not only from film language but from culture, from nuances of words and attitudes. When you translate some totally normal lines from Chinese they sound stupid—why would she ask this question, is she dumb or something?

So when you get down to it, James is usually right. I know I can't win that war and so I'm happy, though sometimes grudgingly, to yield. And through him I've come to understand my own culture a little better. Working with James I get the best of East and West as we bounce back and forth, painfully, sometimes five or six times. What we go through we've done since *Eat Drink Man Woman* in 1994—and it works better with each film, by which I mean I take his idea and make it more authentically Chinese. But by doing this maybe it's also less universal.

NJ: One of the marks of your cinema is still how well it travels.
AL: You find more cultural differences as the working relationship improves. It's not a problem when I do films in English because then James and the crew know what sounds right and Asian audiences are used to reading subtitles, to looking to see if there's something interesting there. But it's harder the other way around, not so much in England as in America where if they don't get it immediately they just cast it aside.

NJ: Did you always have Tony Leung in mind for the role of Mr. Yee?
AL: About a year before I started pre-production I invited him to dinner while he was promoting *2046* in New York. As I talked to him I started to see him as Mr. Yee, even though in reality he's quite the opposite, more like an older character he's played before.

NJ: The film plays off his persona beautifully.
AL: I encouraged him to show his normal self to Wong Chia Chi before

she lets him go. I would like to think there's a traitor or villain deep inside him just like any other person, so everything he does is to cover up what he's longing for. If I had him do menace and poker face, just a villain look, that wouldn't have been any good.

NJ: There's sympathy for him—sympathy for the devil, if you like.
AL: In the introduction to the collection that includes *Lust, Caution*, Eileen Chang wrote that we're probably better off not understanding villains because understanding is the beginning of forgiveness. But you have to bear in mind that as a Chinese writer she often has to put the opposite to what she really wants to say. You can't say, "Oh, she didn't write that sex scene like that so we can't do it" because half of the art of Chinese literature lies in concealment, in not saying what you really mean. I think she loved this guy, so she had to write a very cruel novel and then say that we should not understand him. That's my interpretation, at least.

NJ: Where did you find Tang Wei, the actress who plays Wong Chia Chi?
AL: It's her first movie, and we found her by interviewing ten thousand actresses. I myself saw about a hundred of them, and no one had heard of Tang Wei. She's very close in disposition to how Wong Chia Chi is described in the story—she's like one of my parents' generation, which is pretty rare these days. She didn't seem strikingly beautiful but she did the best reading and there was something about her. Most of all, she's like the female version of me—I identify with her so closely that, by pretending, I found my true self. So the theme of the story has a personal identification for me and I found a vibe of hers that's very close to myself.

Based on a Truly Gay Story

David Colman / 2009

Originally published on Advocate.com, September 2009, and reprinted with permission. Copyright © 2009 Here Media Inc.

Forty years ago this summer, two momentous events happened just one hundred miles apart, but they might as well have been on different planets. Now the *Brokeback Mountain* filmmakers have adapted Elliot Tiber's memoir, *Taking Woodstock,* and imbued Woodstock with the spirit of Stonewall in a controversial new film—and it's a comedy.

In 1969 a pamphlet called the "Gay Scene Guide" bluntly warned visitors of a potential hazard of looking for love in Manhattan's Greenwich Village. "Do not confuse the 'hippy set' with the 'gay set,'" it warned. "There are many hippies in this area, who while they may dress in a 'gay' fashion, are actually quite opposed to any gay advances."

That spring Elliot Tiber needed no such warning. Though the then-thirty-four-year-old decorator was a Greenwich Village habitué, he had almost no interaction with or interest in hippies—their values, their clothes, their music. The only fragment of culture shared by the two factions was, he recalls, "maybe a Janis Joplin song on a jukebox in a gay bar."

Then summer rolled around. Its first real weekend began innocently enough with drinks at the Stonewall Inn, his favorite Christopher Street bar, he says. But when the police showed up for a routine raid, Tiber says, he and the other patrons started to rebel, sparking a riot that brought hundreds of young gay men into Sheridan Square, throwing bottles and overturning police cars. The night changed his life forever.

By contrast, the other happening that summer that Tiber also helped bring to life—the three-day congregation of hippiedom known as Woodstock—seemed to change the world before it even began. The panicked weeks and mounting insanity leading up to the concert, during which

Tiber—through a series of stranger-than-fiction circumstances—came to the festival's rescue by offering a last-minute venue and permit, were the subject of his charming if scattered 2007 memoir, *Taking Woodstock*. Now, with a script by Focus Features CEO James Schamus, the tale has been adapted into an intriguing new film of the same name directed by Ang Lee. Cutting out Stonewall and Tiber's gay city life but reframing the hippie free-love credo to include gays, the film melds the spirit of the two disparate events into one moving tale. Starring breakout comic actor and writer Demetri Martin as Tiber, the film opens August 28.

The film completes a kind of gay trilogy for Lee and Schamus, both of whom, incidentally, are happily married to women. Lee directed *The Wedding Banquet* and *Brokeback Mountain*; Schamus's Focus Features produced *Brokeback* and *Milk*. But it wasn't the memoir's gay main character that first drew Lee to the project, it was Tiber himself; whom Lee first encountered on an early-morning news show.

"I had done six tragedies in a row," Lee says. "The last straw was *Lust, Caution*—that took a lot of out of me. For years I had been wanting to do something more warmhearted, a comedy, and it just happened that when I was promoting *Lust,Caution* in San Francisco, Elliot Tiber was the next guest, and he gave me this two-minute pitch and gave me the book."

The director didn't bite right away, though—and he lost the book. And when Tiber didn't hear back from him, he tracked down Schamus instead and won him over.

Tiber's tenaciousness is easy to imagine. Though he spent a good deal of the past forty years living alternately in New York and Belgium with André Ernotte, a Belgian playwright and director who died in 1999, Tiber, now seventy-four, still comes across as both a born-in-Bensonhurst New Yorker and a curious hybrid of Mae West and Mel Brooks. His outsize life and personality jump off the pages of his book as well, with tales of studying painting with Hans Hofmann, S/M sex with Robert Mapplethorpe, and an ambiguously amorous evening with Marlon Brando, all cropping up before his story even gets upstate. The book contains, as Schamus dryly says, "enough for twenty movies."

But Schamus and Lee decided to focus only on the central thread, dispensing with many of the most blatantly Jewish and gay facets of Tiber's story. (Imagine what the MPAA would have done with a scene of Elliot, who is Jewish, going home with Mapplethorpe from a leather bar to find a mammoth Nazi banner hanging in the photographer's loft—and then still staying the night.)

The story that emerged is like that of Norman Bates with a happy ending: Miserable, eccentric gay man with a crippling sexual self-hatred is saddled with a domineering mother—and her bankrupt hotel—but still ends up saving the day. The similarity to real life ends there. In 1969, Tiber worked in New York City as a decorator and painter and spent his weekends in White Lake, N.Y., in an effort to keep his parents' failing motel afloat with various schemes—a pool! An amateur theater troupe! An annual music festival! All flopped. The motel was on the verge of foreclosure in July, when Tiber happened to read that an actual music festival had just lost its permit in Wallkill, N.Y. So Tiber, who already had a permit for a festival he was planning, picked up the phone and offered his help. That first phone call set off a chain of occurrences: His neighbor's farm became the venue, and his parents' motel was taken over (and the mortgage cares erased) by the event's planners, who made it their headquarters. So too did VW busloads of free spirits, who started arriving in White Lake weeks before the festival's kickoff. The film is essentially a 1930s-style screwball comedy about a drowning man who called for help—and Woodstock showed up.

"The Elliot Tiber in the movie, played by Demetri, was something I think I created with [Schamus]," Lee says, explaining how Tiber's campy persona was transformed for the film version into what comedians call the "straight man." Not a hetero, mind you, but an average guy the audience can identify with as the madness of Woodstock mounts. "We love the idea that our hero is a kind of everyman," Schamus says. "Can't gay men be everymen too?" Lee found a familiar character in the source material, one with whom he is well-acquainted: the passionate but ambivalent person forced by circumstance to make a move or a stand or a choice he doesn't want to, like Bruce Banner filled with radioactive rage in *Hulk* or the conflicted cowboy lovers in *Brokeback Mountain*.

"Americans like heroes," he says. "Americans like people who take sides. That's not so true for me. I identify with these characters trying to keep an absolute balance, who tolerate a lot to keep things safe and all right. These characters cannot make decisions. They're unable to offend anyone. That's their charm and their weakness."

The idea of the music festival as a comedic and miraculous deus ex machina appealed to Lee, who had first started seriously researching Woodstock and the culture that sparked it when he made his 1997 film *The Ice Storm*, which, set among jaded liberals in a Connecticut suburb in 1973, he came to think of as "kind of a hangover from 1969."

But reading about Tiber's experience made him want to explore the idealism that the event represented. In the summer of 1969, Lee was fourteen and living in the highly repressive culture of Taiwan. He recalls kids with long hair being forced off the street to have it shorn. In this world Lee was only dimly aware of hippies and Woodstock, but he had his own growing feelings of being trapped inside and outside of tradition. These feelings only intensified when he decided to be a filmmaker, which won him no approval front his scholarly family. "It was kind of a disgrace," he says. The unfairness and hypocrisy of the system were what he took square aim at with his early comedy *The Wedding Banquet.*

Now, having re-created the festival (on a limited budget and with the help of computer animation that turned 6,000 extras into 500,000), Lee says he still feels the infectious hippie optimism, even more than before he started the film. "They planted the seeds for many good things and pointed out a lot of issues that we take more seriously today," he says. "The fact that half a million people were there and there was no violence is amazing. Something like that will probably never happen again. The idea that the world can be changed overnight, that's the naive part. But the heart and the intention that held it together was quite incredible."

Still, for all of the festival's good points, and for its coincidental timing with the Stonewall rebellion, Lee says he's aware that the demographics and values of Woodstock's attendees had very little overlap with those of the gay rights movement. Only this year, in the revival of the 1967 free-love Broadway hit *Hair,* has the character of Woof been rewritten to be clearly gay. And only recently did the musical's co-creator James Rado reveal that he and his writing partner for the show, Gerome Ragni, were lovers in the 1960s.

Over breakfast in a posh West Village café the morning after Gay Pride, Tiber recalls that when the film was completed, Lee and Schamus organized a screening for him. Schamus and Lee waited outside the screening room for Tiber, and after he exited with his face wet with tears, they asked, "Don't you like it?" Tiber remembers. "I said, 'Are you kidding? It's so beautiful and so moving and so touching.' That's when they told me that they were grateful to tell this story of this gay man with all these problems who not only survived but came out on top and changed the world."

At the end of the film, Elliot, played with wonderful restraint and subdued eccentricity by Martin, bids adieu to his parents and heads off to San Francisco, the land of Harvey Milk and the future of the gay rights movement. In real life Tiber bought a Cadillac and moved to Los Angeles to get a job in the movies. The film's rendering of him is certainly less flamboyant than the true-life man. Sure, the truth is more real—it always is. Though the anger of Stonewall and its bricks and bottles are not in the film, its spirit of liberation is very much felt. As if answering a call, the anarchic joy of Woodstock swoops down to bestow a kiss on a lonely gay frog prince, and it sets him free. However you slice it, it's an awfully nice fairy tale.

Ang Lee Interview for *Taking Woodstock*

John Hiscock / 2009

From the *Telegraph*, October 22, 2009. © Telegraph Media Group Limited 2009.
Reprinted by permission.

Ang Lee was a fourteen-year-old schoolboy preparing for his exams in conservative Taiwan when he saw clips of the Woodstock festival on the television news.

"There were guys with big hair, jamming guitars, a sea of people," he recalled. "I was pretty dull and focused and wasn't particularly cool but I could sense something big was happening." The images stayed with Lee after he moved to America at the age of twenty-four.

"My observation of how America and the world changed meant a lot to me. Over the years Woodstock got glorified and romanticized and became the event that symbolized Utopia," he said. "It's the last page of our collective memory of the age of innocence. Then things turned ugly and would never be the same again." Three months after Woodstock, violence erupted at a music festival featuring the Rolling Stones at Altamont, California, which was policed by Hells Angels and at which four people died.

Lee decided to make a movie about Woodstock's three days of peace, mud, love, and music when he met Elliot Tiber, the man who brought the festival to Max Yasgur's farm in Bethel (not Woodstock) and who was promoting his emotional memoir, *Taking Woodstock*, on a TV talk show.

In adapting the book Lee and his longtime writer-producer partner James Schamus downplayed Tiber's detailed descriptions of his gay explorations in New York City and instead concentrated on the events leading up to the festival. Tiber, whose parents owned a rundown motel in the Catskills in upstate New York, contacted promoter Michael Lang on hearing that a music festival had lost its permit from a neighboring town, and offered the motel to the promoters. Soon Lang's staff was moving into the motel, half a million people were on their way, most of them with more drugs than camping supplies, and Tiber, played by little-known stand-up comic Demetri Martin, found himself swept up in a generation-defining experience that would change his life, and American culture, forever.

"It's not a concert movie; it's about the phenomenon of wanting to go to Woodstock," says Lee. "It's also a story of liberation, honesty, and tolerance—and of a naive spirit that we cannot and must not lose.

"After making several tragic movies in a row, I was looking to do a comedy, and one without cynicism. It might seem a strange idea to make a comedy about Woodstock, but it was kind of bizarre and seemed like comedy material to me." The soundtrack features songs from sixties musical icons including the Grateful Dead, the Doors, Jefferson Airplane, and Country Joe and the Fish, as well as a new recording of "Freedom" from Richie Havens.

Ever since Ang Lee made his first English-language film, an adaptation of Jane Austen's *Sense and Sensibility*, in 1995, actors and critics alike have wondered how the director managed to make such a very English film and then subsequently turn out such quintessentially American ones as *Ice Storm*, *Hulk*, and *Brokeback Mountain*.

Jonathan Groftt, one of the stars of *Taking Woodstock*, found out the hard way. "Research and homework," the young actor says succinctly. "The first time I met him he dropped this huge, four-inch thick, three-ring binder down on the desk. Bam! And he said, 'Are you ready to do your homework? This is just the beginning.'"

Grofft, who portrays Lang, the laid-back instigator of the festival, also had to read a dozen books, listen to a pile of cds prescribed by Lee and watch fifteen movies.

Lee, fifty-four, was equally demanding of the extras, sending them all to "hippy camp" where they were given a "hippy handbook" to read containing a compendium of articles, timelines, essays, and a glossary of "hippie lingo," from "freak out" to "roach clip." They were drilled in the language, attitude, and politics of 1969 and shown documentaries about the time period, with Lee paying particular attention to the way they moved and looked.

"In the body posture and the way they look at each other is an implicit understanding of cool and connection," said Lee, in his occasionally disjointed English. "I had to make sure they had it. Their muscles were different and thinner, and the women who expose themselves on film had to be cast two months ahead of time so they could grow their hair.

"I found the biggest difference between youth then and youth today was that today's kids seem to have more purpose in their eyes. Even though they do cool things, they know where they are going. But back then there was this de-focused, rebellious kind of a thing and I just wanted to make sure they were not too energetic but were mellow."

Ever since Lee gained international attention with his second feature, *The Wedding Banquet*, in 1993, about a gay Taiwanese man who marries to please his parents, his films have defied pigeonholing.

"I like to think I'm un-categorizable," he laughed. "I guess I've been kind of an outsider—an alien—all my life." After his paternal grandparents were executed for being landowners during the Cultural Revolution in China, his father, a scholar and school headmaster, fled to Taiwan where Ang was born. After studying acting in Taipei he moved to the U.S., attended college at the University of Illinois, and then began his moviemaking career at New York University film school.

"The Cultural Revolution didn't really affect me but it had a big impact on my father, of course," he said. "His roots were basically pulled out and it was an overwhelming, life-changing experience for him. I grew up pretty much prevented from knowing anything from Communist China except that they were the bad guys that stole our country. The biggest impact on me when I came to the United States was that I had a chance to actually read communist books." Short films he made earned him an agent but he spent five years struggling to get projects off the ground, while looking after his two sons while his wife, microbiologist Janice Lin, was the family breadwinner.

After *The Wedding Banquet*, he made *Eat Drink Man Woman*, which picked up an Oscar nomination for best foreign-language film. Then came *Sense and Sensibility*, which received seven Oscar nominations. His directing style prompted the producer, Lindsay Doran, to comment at the time: "British actors are used to directors who are either mean and rude or gentle and nice; but having a director who's gentle and nice but also rude was a new experience for them."

His *Crouching Tiger, Hidden Dragon*, earned ten Oscar nominations and won for best foreign-language film, but his follow-up film, *Hulk*, was not a success and was decried as too unrealistic and cartoony-looking.

Lee finally won a best directing Oscar for *Brokeback Mountain*, the story of a homosexual love affair which spanned several decades.

He has no firm plans for his next project but whatever it is, he will undoubtedly immerse himself in it totally.

"I probably can root and identify more with the movie I'm making than with life," he said. "That fictionalized world seems to make more sense than the real world, because it has a beginning, middle, and end. It gives meaning and wisdom and it's easier for me to live there than in the real world.

"I guess that's kind of abstract, but that's how it is."

Crossing Borders

Glenn Kenny / 2010

From *DGA Quarterly* 4, no. 1 (Spring 2010). Permission to reprint courtesy of the Directors Guild of America, Inc.

"It's a good day to do an interview," says Ang Lee on a quiet morning in midtown Manhattan. The director is in a brief lull as he moves from one office to another before embarking on his latest cinematic adventure. So the space where we meet is relatively empty, and though Lee is low key and serene, it is his formidable presence that fills the room.

There is a paradox at work here. Despite his mild manner, Lee has been something of an artistic daredevil, flying from one genre to another and consistently taking risks. With his still controversial *Hulk*, he tried to bring genuine human feeling to a comic bock superhero; with *Lust, Caution*, the lineaments of the erotic thriller was applied to something deeper, more profound. His last feature, *Taking Woodstock*, was a coming-of-age story set against the counterculture upheaval of the sixties, which doesn't sound particularly subversive, except when you consider it was as much a coming-out story as it was a coming-of-age story.

Born in Taiwan, Lee has directed an impressively varied array of humanist films, including *The Wedding Banquet, Eat Drink Man Woman, The Ice Storm*, and *Ride with the Devil*. He was nominated for a DGA Award for his Jane Austen adaptation, *Sense and Sensibility*, and won DGA Awards for *Crouching Tiger, Hidden Dragon* and *Brokeback Mountain*, for which he also received the Academy Award for best director.

Listening to Lee describe his working methods, one is struck by the compassion of his vision. He said he was honored to do the DGA Interview, and seemed to regard the occasion as a chance to articulate his artistic principles—not just for members, but for himself. "It's great," he says, "to have gotten to a place where I can share advice and experience with my fellows in this way."

Glenn Kenny: In a sense you are both a Taiwanese filmmaker and an American one. So let's start by talking about your beginnings and how you got to this place.

Ang Lee: In Taiwan I was brought up very non-artistically. The idea in my family, in the culture itself, was to study something practical, get into a good college, then come to America and study, get a degree. But I flunked the college examination because I was too nervous. I got into the Taiwan University of Art, majoring in theater and cinema. Back then, in the early seventies, there was not much you could do with cinema in Taiwan. But once I stood on stage, as an actor, I just fell in love. I was very happy at the school but we didn't have a lot of Western theater. I started watching a lot of movies—Bergman, Renoir, many movies by these masters. At the age of twenty-three, I got into the University of Illinois, majoring in theater. I had two years there. That changed my life; I started to devour Western culture, not so much literature or science or social studies, but theater.

Q: At what point did you realize you were more interested in directing than acting?

A: It happened when I started studying in the States. I couldn't speak much English at all, I spoke pidgin English. And because of that I couldn't really act. So I switched from acting to directing. Nevertheless, I think I absorbed a lot that changed me. I grew up in an agricultural culture, which tries to emphasize peace and balance with society and nature, and so attempts to diffuse as much conflict as it can. But in Western culture, particularly theatrical culture, it's all about conflict, asserting personal free will and how that can create a conflict within the family, or in the larger society. And I found I was talented at communicating those kinds of situations. Eventually, after all my exposure to film, seeing five to seven movies every weekend, I wanted to do films. I did my graduate work at NYU, three years in the film program. It's a very pragmatic program; you just go out and make movies.

Q: So how did you make the transition from student to professional?

A: Well, after film school, I went through six years of development hell. At NYU we did short films, and I got an agent at William Morris based on those. The thing was, after getting out, it took me three years to really understand the difference between a short and a feature. Nobody really taught us how to deal with a feature-length structure, how that functions, how to develop characters. So now I was lost again. I did quite a bit of pitching in Hollywood, and one project after another just kept falling apart. But through those years I was able to teach myself a few things. Among them, how a feature-length script functions, and what the market wants.

Q: How did you finally break through?

A: In 1990 I entered a Taiwanese government script competition. It was good money, $16,000 for first prize, and half that amount for second place. And I won both first and second place! The first was for *Pushing Hands*. I just wrote it specifically for the competition. And *The Wedding Banquet*, which I had written five years before, won the second prize, and that became my second film. When I wrote *Wedding Banquet*, it was too Chinese to make in the U.S. and too gay to make in Taiwan. So it had just been sitting there. So I sent the two scripts in and both won. And then a Taiwanese studio wanted to invest in *Pushing Hands*. It was a small story of a Taiwanese family set in New York. They gave me about $400,000 to make the movie in New York. I was referred to Good Machine, the production company started by Ted Hope and James Schamus. I pitched the story to them, and James said to me, "No wonder you couldn't get anything made for six years. You're the worst pitcher—you can't pitch out of a basket." They pitched themselves to me as the kings of no-budget filmmaking. Not low budget, no budget. So we hooked up, did the first movie and it was a hit in Taiwan. It didn't go anywhere else, really. And because that was a hit, the Taiwan studio gave me more money, three-quarters of a million, to make *The Wedding Banquet*. James said, "Let me help you revise the script." He did, and the rest, I would like to say, is history.

Q: That started your partnership with Schamus, who has co-written and co-produced almost all of the ten films you've made since 1993, and as head of Focus Features, distributed several of them as well. How has that relationship helped make it possible for you to keep up a steady output of films?

A: It has been a very organic partnership, something that came out of a friendship, not any kind of master plan. *The Wedding Banquet* was seen by the future producers of *Sense and Sensibility*, and because of that film, somehow they thought I'd be a good candidate to adapt Jane Austen. I turned to James and asked, "What am I going to do?" During that time we were thinking about doing English-language films with each other. But these producers approached with *Sense*, and I couldn't decide whether to do it or not; for one thing the budget was $16 million. I had never handled that kind of money. And also, I had never done a period piece. But I just couldn't refuse the temptation to work with Emma Thompson. I read the script [written by Thompson] and despite my English being less fluent at the time, I felt I knew it by heart, that by its nature it was very close to what I do. So I took the challenge, and I went to England. I was very scared. I spoke broken English, and there was Jane Austen. I had to work with a top-of-the-line English cast and crew, with Oxforders, Royal Shakespeareans—just a top-notch cast and crew. Of course I was going to feel intimidated. So I brought James along with me. And during this time and through the shoot, James became kind of my frontman, doing the social interaction with all these people while I was doing my thing.

Q: After *Sense and Sensibility*, you jumped to *The Ice Storm*, about the mores of a totally different society: America in the early seventies. How did that project come about?
A: I read the book because James had recommended it; I wasn't necessarily looking to make a movie of it. But when I read the part where the character Mikey Carver is sliding down the ice, that image just clicked in my head. I told James, "I think I want to make this into a movie." He thought it was a valid idea, and then we met [the author of the book] Rick Moody. We bought the rights for nearly nothing. *Sense and Sensibility* interrupted that process, but when we picked it up again, that was the first time James wrote a screenplay for me on his own.

Q: After establishing yourself in this country with *The Ice Storm*, you then went back to China for *Crouching Tiger, Hidden Dragon*. What was that like?
A: I was directing both in English and Chinese and bouncing in between the two: it became a balancing act for me. In American films, because it was an adopted culture, the skill and artistic endeavor became clearer. And actually in some ways, psychologically it's easier. I see the subtext better. As a foreigner, accuracy is the first thing you'll see, but getting the cultural habits is more difficult. Then once I had directed in English and went back and started *Crouching Tiger*, I found my thinking had been Westernized, globalized a lot. So I had to find my way back into the Chinese culture, which was my first culture.

Q: In your career, you've gone from a Civil War tale, a superhero adaptation, a modern-day Western. What do you think makes you jump from genre to genre?

A: I have this fear that if I stay in one place, I will lose the freshness I like to bring to every film. If I stay in one genre, I'm afraid I'll be less honest, because having a certain kind of fluency in a particular genre might allow me to, I don't know, to fake it. I feel that in order to do my best work I have to put myself in a place where I don't know much about what I'm doing. A place where I could feel as if I were making my first movie. If I feel like I'm repeating something, or repeating myself, I actually feel more frightened than I would in taking the risk of doing something new.

Q: Is that why you change cinematographers periodically?

A: I think it's potentially interesting to have a relationship with somebody over a few movies in a row that keeps developing, goes deeper and deeper and becomes more and more artistically fruitful. With cinematographers, there are a few principles I think I stick to. And when I get hooked up with them, it's for a specific reason. I approached Frederick Elmes for *The Ice Storm* because the last part of that story, the most important part of it, is the stormy night when the power goes out, the lights go off. The cinematographer was going to have to create this illusion of letting us see people function in the dark. That's the core of the drama. I so admired what Fred did with David Lynch, particularly in *Blue Velvet*. Fred just pushed it to the maximum of how low the exposure could get, and he does these wonderful, experimental things.

Q: What about your visual approach for *Brokeback Mountain*?

A: I went for Rodrigo Prieto [*Amores Perros*, *Babel*] on *Brokeback Mountain* because I think he's versatile, and I wanted somebody who could shoot quickly. But then I asked him to do the opposite of the frenetic style that he is famous for and he was able to give me the tranquil, almost passive look I wanted for *Brokeback*. I believe a talent's a talent.

Q: How do you collaborate with your cinematographer?

A: I like to work with a cinematographer who has two distinct attitudes, regardless of age or experience. First, I want them to talk to me about the drama, not the visuals. I'm not worried about how to shoot it. That will come along if we focus on how to help the actors portray the characters, and move in a way in which they can perform comfortably. I want the cinematographer to have an interest in the content, in telling the story. That's number one for me. And number two: I don't want anyone who's going to behave as if he or she is a master, someone who knows everything about what they do. I want to work with someone who feels they're still learning, who doesn't automatically have all the answers. When I meet with someone and ask them what they think about something, and they're not sure, that's usually a good sign for me.

Q: A couple of your films have strong visual effects elements—*Crouching Tiger, Hidden Dragon*, with the wirework that gives its characters the appearance of flying, and *Hulk* with CGI animating a comic book character. How do you retain the humanity of your characters when working with these effects?

A: Well you know, wirework is actually a relatively low-tech special effect, and there's no way of getting away from the human element of it. For *Crouching Tiger*'s battle in the bamboo forest, we had scores of people on the ground physically manipulating the various elements. The human aspect as far as the characters were concerned had to do with the way they fly, which was not specified in the writing but conceived and carried out in the shooting. For instance, Zhang Ziyi's character seems to be able to fly at will, while the older character played by Michelle Yeoh is a very fast runner, and the momentum she gains by running enables her to bounce up. These particular techniques were very expressive of what the characters were about.

Q: How was that different on *Hulk*?

A: On *Hulk* I looked at it as if I were a painter and was using a new and very expensive tool. It was problematic commercially, because what we made was more of a horror movie than a comic book movie, and we had to sell it like *Spider-Man*. For me, the theme was tied in with that of *Crouching Tiger*. In that film, the "hidden dragon" is what's inherent but also repressed in the culture—so in the East it was sex; in *Hulk*'s America the "hidden dragon" is anger and violence. But we found that instead of describing what I wanted to the animators, if I put on the motion-capture suit or let them shoot my face acting out a certain expression, it could save them weeks of work. So I wound up performing the actions of the *Hulk*, acting out his anger. And it was a very profound experience for me. I like to work with CGI in a way that the audience won't see. We actually used some CGI on *Brokeback Mountain*, with some of the landscapes. If you want a cloud to be in a particular place in the image, you can just put it there. It's wonderful.

Q: Do you regret not having access to today's special effects tools when you made *The Ice Storm*, which required certain specific images?
A: No, we were able to get what we needed. This is the important thing: people watch a movie, and a movie's average length is something like an hour and forty minutes, two hours. And I believe that people really focus on the film as an image for maybe about ten, fifteen minutes. The drama is what is really important in the kinds of films I make. It's got to be about human beings. Nothing holds your attention longer than human faces, something the audience can identify with. Storytelling, drama, and human faces—all those comprise the center of what I want to do. I spent movie after movie trying to break away from it, to be more visual, because I like differences. But you can only do so much. It all has to relate to the characters.

Q: One of the most dramatic moments in all your work is the scene when Ennis Del Mar visits Jack Twist's parents at the end of *Brokeback Mountain*. How did you go about setting the mood?
A: Well, it goes much farther back from the point when you step on the set. And that scene is, as it happens, my favorite scene in the movie. It's a very stoic scene, a scene about a person who's not there but had been brought to life so vividly by Jake Gyllenhaal, who all of these characters have lost. For my visual inspiration I referred to Andrew Wyeth, and also the Danish painter Vilhelm Hammershoi, for those stark, white doors. So the first thing to do was find the right house, the right space, and of course that's the task I brought to the production designer, Judy Becker. And to shoot that scene I used a style that I had worked with in *Hulk*. I shot with two cameras, capturing the actors from both sides, and then changing lenses and doing it again. It's a very irregular way of coverage. When you edit it together, you can apply certain emphasis to certain reactions, emotions. Shooting this kind of coverage can confuse some actors. But of course it did not confuse Heath [Ledger], Peter [McRobbie], and Roberta [Maxwell], all of whom I just loved. It was a strange day. I wanted a lot of sunshine for that scene, and I got it, and I remember walking to the set and just feeling that this was going to be a great day. Still, a scene like that, it's the actors and their faces, they make it all.

Q: In casting, you frequently mix experienced actors with novices. How do you guide actors to give you the emotion you need for each film?
A: I probably can talk about this for days, because every actor is different. And each one is like a mountain you have to climb over. Nothing,

of course, is easy. I think when one devotes so much energy in making a movie, at the very least the leading roles are a significant part of you as the director. So you apply yourself to the actors.

And they know that. You're watching them, they're watching you. And I'm wondering, how can I turn them into something I had in mind? And they're watching me, trying to figure out a part of my mind, so they can play that. It's all very abstract and it goes back and forth a lot. I've said about my relations with cinematographers, production designers, writers, and producers, that I give them all parts of myself. But I have no doubt I give my best part to actors. It doesn't mean that I'm a friend of theirs. I hardly, if ever, socialize with them. Some of them have found me cold, in fact. But I do what I think I have to in order to get artistic moments laid out and fixed on celluloid for good. There's definitely a battle to it. Making a movie is pretty holy to me, and I think the actors sense that.

Q: Is it ever a problem getting a newcomer and a veteran on the same page?

A: It can be difficult getting everything on the same page. When I did *Sense and Sensibility*, Kate Winslet was only nineteen, it was her second movie. It could be difficult to get her to do certain things, to deal with the camera and not to react to it self-consciously. Now, of course, she is aware of all that, but not so much back then. And that's the easiest thing for Emma Thompson, on top of which, Emma can deliver something like four or five layers of meaning at once, effortlessly. While Kate, even at that relatively raw stage, had the power to move people, to make the audience worry for her. That seemed like an easy thing for Kate, and a harder thing for Emma. And they were playing sisters.

Q: What's the process like when you're just beginning to work with the actors?

A: First off, you have to get a sense of their breathing, their vibes. Rehearsing helps you get into the zone. But the most important thing is the shooting day. Usually I do two, three weeks of rehearsal. The rehearsal is not about running through the film like it's the real thing. I think movie actors tend not to give you a lot during rehearsals, and for good reason. Because if they give it all out, you lose it for the shooting days. If they hold it, then those qualities you're really looking for are—we hope—preserved for the shooting. So I think rehearsals are about helping us all to see the actors, and for myself, to see and hear the character begin to take shape in them, to have a taste of the character and that character's chemistry with the others. On set, we all have to work with the camera and we work for the moments. You have to think and feel. And so what comes out of the rehearsal is not the performance, but a way of thinking together.

Q: With all of this activity going on around you, how do you see your role as director?

A: I think film is an artificial medium. It's not life. It's not real. But it certainly has a god of its own. There's a film god you have to worship. There's a certain point you just have to give up everybody's ideas and listen to that voice. I initiate a lot of things, but then I kind of become the observer and decide which way to go that will match the film god's intent. I think each film has its own way. I tell my cast and crew it's not about us, it's not about me. We're all slaves to that big master of the movies. So that's my goal. I try to tune everybody in to that and bring unity.

Q: What's the first thing you do when you come on the set?

A: When I'm shooting, I block in the morning, and then the actors go back to do their makeup. I give out the shot list. I work out the upcoming scene with the assistant director, the camera person, and the art department. And when we have the shot ready, we work on the details, refine them. And try to hit, hit, hit until you hit that one take, take after take.

Q: How many takes?

A: I would say six or seven. It's hard to go over twelve takes. Probably no less than three takes. On *Lust, Caution*, after five takes Tang Wei, who was making her first film, would lose concentration. She was very emotional, very moody. She would zoom into the mood of the set right away, but then she might drift. With other similarly less experienced actors it's different. Leehom Wang [in *Lust, Caution*] or Demetri Martin [in *Taking Woodstock*], both novice film actors, would consistently get better take after take. You could count on the seventh take being better than the sixth. But by the same token, you also really haven't gotten anywhere until the fifth take. And then you have a dream actor like a Tony Leung [*Lust, Caution*] or a Joan Allen [*The Ice Storm*], and take after take they're just perfect. So you have all of that. There's a lot of mixing, matching, and balancing to do.

Q: In *Lust, Caution* you combined emotional intensity with very explicit sex scenes. Was it difficult to get the right balance?

A: Yes. The two characters are trying to kill each other. He's an interrogator and she is the seducer, and I don't find anything more intense than that. With actors I get into subject matter I don't even get into with my wife, with my family, because I share the most private place with the actors and am very direct with them. We make our art out of those materials and we make a connection at that level. And with those characters I was exposing myself. So that was a very painful experience for me actually. With the sex scenes, I think we were breaking the boundaries of certain kinds of acting. To oversee that, to create a situation where you have to wonder whether what's going on in front of you is real, that's the ultimate experience that a director can have with actors. But it was terrible, too. After the shoot we all got sick for a month. It was that intense. And after the movie, for the first time, I felt it was my job to bring the actors back from it. I'm still dealing with Tang Wei. I'm still helping her to come off from that character. In the past I didn't see that as my job.

Q: What kind of relationship do you usually have with your actors?

A: I don't know how actors feel about me. I used to be able to get away with certain things when I first directed English-language movies. Because I couldn't speak English very well, I'd give very direct and blunt directions. The actors would be shocked by this, but they figured it was because my English was bad and I didn't know any better, so they tolerated it. But the better my English became, the less I could get away with it. I had to become more civilized like everybody else. With *Taking Woodstock* I began to loosen up a bit, partially because the process of making *Lust, Caution* was so intense. Aside from the sunnier subject matter, I personally decided to be a little nicer, a little more complimentary, and be more concerned with making sure everybody was happy.

Q: Some of your pictures seem to be designed for an international audience. Have they been well received overseas, especially in the Asian market?

A: Our experiences with Asian markets have been interesting. When we made *Crouching Tiger, Hidden Dragon*, it was because for a long time I had wanted to make a martial arts film, but at the same time I thought I had to upgrade it. I didn't want to just make a Hong Kong–style B-genre movie of the type I saw when I was growing up. We wound up giving it a mixture of A and B ingredients. That didn't really go over very well in the

Eastern markets, although we had great success in the West. The fresh approach was more appreciated here. The opposite happened with *Lust, Caution*. It was a huge cultural phenomenon in the East, but it didn't do anything in the West. Maybe because it related so directly to history there, and maybe because its sense of tragedy is more commonly accepted in the East than it is here.

Q: What's the audience like in China?
A: Mainland Chinese cinema is really beginning to lake off. It's a new market and it's an interesting market, and that industry is beginning to make its own middle-of-the-road movies. Piracy is everywhere but the audience there still goes to the movie theater. Looking at what becomes a hit there, even for me it's very hard to understand why they like certain things, why they don't like certain things. But they're four times the size of the American audience, so even just playing one city, a film can make a hundred million, and it's a hit. That's a significant market.

Q: Given the complexities of the marketplace, do you think there will continue to be room for the kind of films you make?
A: I'm in a pretty safe zone. When I'm making what you might call a big-small movie, I don't particularly have much of a problem then. And I get to make the movie I want to make. In terms of international movies, I think there are a lot of interesting movies that happen outside of America. And the American art house film seems to be defined as a low-budget enterprise. So you have that, and then there's the Hollywood movie. But I do think we need a lot more of what you might call the "tweeners." Movies are being polarized. You have some successful directors of artistic integrity who get to do more expensive movies, but not a lot of them.

Q: Your next film, *The Life of Pi*, based on the book by Yann Martel, is an adventure story about a boy stranded on a lifeboat in the Pacific with a zebra, a hyena, an orangutan, and a tiger. That sounds like a tricky film that will require lots of preparation.
A: I was very intrigued by the book when I read it in 2001 but didn't think it could be made into a movie. Then when I was starting *Woodstock*, Fox 2000 approached me and said the project had become available again. This movie I think will be different because technically it's difficult. It deals with animation, so previsualization will come into play. I hate previsualization, usually I don't do storyboards. Sometimes I do, but I don't follow them. Why would you cover the shot [as it was storyboarded]

instead of finding something and trying to make that work for you? It doesn't make much sense to me. But then directing doesn't stand still. When you do shots that are expensive, you have to plan them out. You cannot afford the usual process. It's exciting. It's moviemaking. There are no rules.

Spinning Platters Interview: Ang Lee on *Life of Pi*

Jason LeRoy / 2012

From SpinningPlatters.com, November 26, 2012. Reprinted by permission.

They said it couldn't be done: a movie version of Yann Martel's bestselling novel *Life of Pi*, an intensely visual parable that consists almost entirely of a teenaged Indian boy named Pi lost at sea on a tiny rowboat with a wild tiger as his only companion? Bah, said some. Blergh, exclaimed others. Bloop, said NeNe Leakes. But clearly the naysayers hadn't considered the possibility that Ang Lee, the Oscar-winning fifty-eight-year-old director of such contemporary classics as *Crouching Tiger, Hidden Dragon* and *Brokeback Mountain*, would consider taking the helm. But take it he did, choosing the spiritual allegory as his follow-up to the modestly received *Taking Woodstock*.

Lee is a man who clearly gets off on massive challenges. Not only did he choose an actor with no previous experience (Suraj Sharma) for the lead role, but to tell Martel's intimate yet larger-than-life story, he pushed film technology to the most cutting of edges by creating an almost entirely digital visual wonderland for the film's various fantastical settings (and in 3D, no less). The resulting movie combines astoundingly gasp-inducing visuals with an uncompromisingly spiritual and philosophical framework, anchored by Suraj's remarkable performance. It is difficult to imagine any director other than Lee realizing this challenging material on such a grand and meticulous scale. Below, Lee sits down with Spinning Platters to discuss the root of his passion for storytelling, which of his *Crouching Tiger* characters he channeled for *Life of Pi*'s tiger, and getting to take advantage of new actors.

Jason LeRoy: Each new film you make seems so different from those you've made before. What was it about *Life of Pi* that appealed to you?

Ang Lee: It's advertised as a story that will make you believe in God, but of course no one is going to buy that. It's actually about the ideas of believing and stories. I'm a storyteller; I make movies. So it's really changed the essence of what I do, the illusions I create: how they affect our lives, how we take them as real, how they are even more important in some ways than reality. To me, that's the truth. I make movies about people in false situations who devote so much emotion to it they get lost, such as in *Lust, Caution*. That subject matter really haunts me. I wanted to make the movie also because of the voyage part, which is really vividly and visually written. If you could make it happen, it would be wonderful movie material.

The part in India, even though it's a lot of material and you have to narrow it down before you sink the ship—it's challenging in terms of length, but it's very colorful. And then it has a philosophical ending. That's the tough part, that's a challenge. I looked forward to it and I cannot say I enjoyed doing it. [*laughs*] But it's haunting. It's philosophical questions that haunt me. I like to put in my own two cents. I want to do what the book does, but with the cinema. In my opinion it's harder doing cinema than a book, because cinema is more direct. It's a photo-realistic image right in front of your face. What you see is what it is. How do you do that? How do you discuss the illusion you're watching inside of an illusion? That's a great challenge to me. That's enough reason to do it, isn't it? Except it's a big dice to roll, for me and for everybody else involved. But I think at the end it's worth it. [*laughs*]

JL: Many of your previous films have also been about people throwing themselves into extreme situations, and they all seem to feature some sort of metaphysical element, whether most obviously in *Hulk* or even the psychotropic drugs in *Taking Woodstock*. But in *Life of Pi*, there's a really overt dialogue about religion and faith. Was that something that lured you toward it or pushed you away? Because here the vehicle is so obvious, while in your other films it hasn't been.

AL: As I said, nobody will watch the movie or read the book and start believing in God if they don't. It's not that. That's the overt part. If there's a deeper metaphor, I'm not supposed to tell you. [*laughs*] Of course there are other parts that are not so obvious. The biggest challenge I have is making a movie that gives people hope and faith, because that's very important to us. But there's also Pi's frustration, his anger, his confusion; and not to mention, there's a second story. I think that's the provocative part, that they coexist in the movie. I think it depends on how people take things away from the movie, whether they go for the first story or the second story. There are many ways to look at the movie, and my job is to provide chances for everybody [to connect with it], not particularly the faithful, atheists, younger kids who can take the adventure story, or people who enjoy philosophical thinking or metaphorical contemplation. They can all do that. I don't know if I reached it, but that certainly is the goal. And that's no different than any other movie I've made. I think good movies should have that.

JL: What was your familiarity with the book prior to signing on?

AL: Somebody recommended it to me and I read it, then I recommended it to my wife and kids. I didn't think I would want to make it into a movie, but as a filmmaker it haunted me. As I said, we talk about illusions and how real you can make them, and if that is actually the essence of reality. That really haunts me, and some of the images haunted me. But I thought it would be too expensive to do justice to the book, and technically I didn't think we were ready. Even today it was very challenging. So until they approached me with the project about five years ago, it was an interesting idea in the back of my head but I never really thought about pursuing it.

JL: One of the main changes from the novel is having Pi recount the story directly to Yann. How did that come about?

AL: That's one of the first ideas I had. It's a weird book! How do you make that into a structural movie? That's the first thing I thought when I was deciding whether to do this: it doesn't matter how fantastical the voyage is. Unless you find a structure, you cannot tell the story or go about making the movie. I noticed in the prologue, this Indian guy tells Yann, "There's a guy in Canada with a story that will make you believe in God." That's pretty funny, and he went [to Canada], so I thought, "Okay, that's a joke from Yann Martel, so let me take it seriously like it really happened." I get a kick out of it! I thought that was a good way to structure the movie.

Even though the book is a sixteen-year-old boy's journey, I found that it was told in a very mature voice, so it has to be told by a mature person rather than a kid. The kid can fill in the blanks with voiceovers from his diary, but the majority of his explanation has to come from an older voice. And this is material that deals with the power of storytelling and sharing and listening, so I thought, "Well, that's a good tool. Pi will tell the story, then the writer will take over the story and create the book." I'm using fiction as a reality.

JL: Since this is so much about the power of stories and storytelling, do you remember any of the first stories that inspired you to become a storyteller?

AL: [*pause*] Movies, probably. My mother is not a particularly good storyteller, and my father never told me a story except something happened to him. But they have story elements in them. I went to Catholic kindergarten and my mother took me to church, so there are a lot of stories there. But I think movies probably the most, stories told by images. I had a three-years-younger brother, and for years every day I would tell him many stories. I would just make up stories and he would listen. That's how we spent our childhood: me telling stories to my younger brother. I don't know why we did that and I don't know why he would listen, but I guess I just liked to be a storyteller. More so than a listener, probably.

JL: The tiger is such a pivotal character in the novel. How did you approach realizing it for the film and conveying its personality?

AL: I learned about tiger behavior, and there's only so many things a real tiger would do. I didn't want to go outside of that. I'm not gonna have it talk or stare at you like it loves you; I'm not gonna humanize it. But as a character, it's not like building with an actor because I never actually see the tiger. It's either some real tiger who's trained to do something and you're scared of him, or it's entirely digital and you just create him out of your imagination. So when I go about it personally I think I'm dealing with my Crouching Tiger inside, something I'm creating and imagining. I have a few experiences with such characters.

The closest I could think of, even though it's a human being, is the Jen character in *Crouching Tiger, Hidden Dragon*, the part Zhang Ziyi plays. If I see something I'm familiar with, if I know such a person, I wipe away that idea. I want to create something. I'm imagining something totally fascinating to me, for her to go the complete opposite of what I want her to do and be totally rebellious. And that girl will fly, and they couldn't catch her; Mu Bai to his death couldn't touch her, except as the Hidden Dragon. So I worked with Zhang Ziyi and created that character I think quite vividly. I don't know anyone even close to her, and that's my idea of a character. I went about the character of the tiger like that, except I worked a lot harder and thousands of people assisted me in digitally creating it over a year and a half. In principal they are similar, but this one was a lot harder. [*laughs*]

JL: In addition to the myriad technical challenges, you have a first-time actor playing your lead. And not only is Suraj a first-time actor, but due to the digital nature of the filmmaking, was he essentially acting in a void for most of his scenes?
AL: That's why he is such a talent. You sit, there's a blue man there who's supposed to be the tiger, and you just act this way and that way. The water part he had to negotiate with himself. That's all real; if he fumbles, he fumbles. For the tiger part, the situation where he faces God spiritually, he has to put himself in the situation. If I don't see it, I don't see it and he has to try again. In that way he's no different than an experienced actor. But in some ways, a fresh and less-experienced actor has more innocence that you can rip off and take advantage of. [*laughs*] They don't know other ways to make movies and they don't have cynicism; when they're in, they're in. In some ways it's easier than an experienced jaded actor. He was a gift from God in making this movie. He's convincing; he invests his belief in the situation and then we believe in it. I'm a talented filmmaker, so if I see it I know whether he believes or not. I could tell, so I would just tell him to keep trying.

My direction to him was very direct. "You don't look like you're scared." Old tricks like if you breathe harder you'll sense it more. But eventually he has to believe the thing. He's a talented actor and has no trouble believing things. Sometimes he cries and it's heartbreaking. The scene where he's stroking the tiger's head in his lap is so heartbreaking, but all he was holding was a big sandbag. He's performing to a blue sandbag! He said he might not be able to do it because we were near a crowded schoolyard and he was very distracted by the noise, but then he did it on the third take. People were very affected. The makeup woman was like his surrogate mother on the set, and she was like, [*sobbing*] "I'm a proud mother!" He's a talent.

JL: So what's next for you?
AL: Nothing. I'm going to collapse after I'm done promoting this movie. [*laughs*]

Interview: Ang Lee on the Journey of Bringing *Life of Pi* to the Screen

Alex Billington / 2012

From FirstShowing.net, December 18, 2012. Reprinted by permission.

Now playing in 3D in theaters everywhere is one of my favorite films of the year, *Life of Pi*, directed by Oscar-winning Taiwanese filmmaker Ang Lee. I gave the film a 9/10 in my review, and Jeremy went all out with 10/10, because it's really about the wonderful magic of cinema, and what filmmakers can do with the right storytelling tools, including even 3D. Ang Lee is a diverse filmmaker of many acclaimed hits like *Crouching Tiger, Hidden Dragon*, *Sense and Sensibility*, *Brokeback Mountain*, *Lust, Caution*, and even *Hulk*. I was lucky enough to be given a chance to sit down with Ang for twenty minutes in New York City a few weeks ago for a discussion on bringing the wondrous story *Life of Pi* to the big screen.

This was taped at a hotel and could not be recorded on video, so here's the full transcription of my Ang Lee interview on *Life of Pi*. I wrote about the film: "There are minor lulls and downtime as we follow Pi and his struggles on the lifeboat, but they're worth getting through for moments of sheer fascination and celluloid joy. The kind of moments that remind us 'This is why I go to the movies' and also 'this is why I love them.'"

Alex Billington: How did you know how to approach this story as a movie? Did you read Yann Martel's book and immediately think, "This is exactly what want to do?" Was it an evolution?

Ang Lee: I read the book when it first came out. I was fascinated by it. It was also mind boggling and all of that. It's not even close to making as a movie. That's pretty obvious. And then four or five years ago Fox approached me. Then I started thinking, "How do I crack this?" Then I started to gradually get hooked. I thought if I had a structure . . . 'cause this is a story that examines the power of storytelling, which is what I do, examine illusion. The movie relies so much on illusion—how do you give the audience an emotional ride?—which is not what the book is about. It's a philosophical book. How do you give them an emotional ride and then examine the illusion within the illusion of a movie? I think that's kind of unsolvable.

Then I thought Older Pi [will] tell the story. So you have the third person and the first person. So maybe that will work. Then I thought of 3D, which is a very naive idea, because like four years ago I had no idea. I just thought maybe with adding another dimension, maybe, just maybe . . . maybe things will open up. Then I got hooked [*laughs*] little by little. It's a long effort. The script took about a year, and then I took another year to do pre-visualization. Then I did my homework. Then I had to think out of the box, because to do a water movie you have to create a water tank, because I've never seen a movie do a water tank well. It's like I have to top it. I've got to dissolve it and I've got to come further along with that surge. How do I do that? I thought, "There's no way I can do it in LA." Then I thought of Taiwan. It's a long process.

But I did my study. I thought 3D would look really good with water. Just little by little. Still, I think after all the problems were solved, the first thing I mentioned was still the hardest thing, is how do you wrap it up, without throwing your audience off the track, so to speak? That's really hard—how to bring up the second [half], how to conclude.

Billington: Speaking of the ending, I wanted to ask about why you felt it was important to include the modern-day book ends with the third-person author telling the story.

Lee: Because the third person, it gives meaning. He had thirty years to think about it, chew on it, gnaw on it, spit it back in a weird way. And you don't know what is coming. Because the book is mostly told by a mature voice. I don't know, a thirty-five-year-old Canadian; I don't know what that is, but it's quite mature and philosophical. That doesn't belong to a sixteen-year-old Indian boy. So I thought an older voice is necessary. Then because of the thinking book, but you want to stay in the feelings, so it has to be the same person, not another writer or just some weird voiceover. And you cannot do a voice about a young . . . there is another way to do it—Young Pi tell the first story in the infirmary, in the hospital, to the Japanese. And naturally, that's how you would go about it, but the voice wouldn't be right. And because it's him, it's the same person, emotionally you cannot really detach.

So I thought—a third person, sort of an omnipresent objective point of view, but at the same time it's the same person, will be the solution. That's how I came about the framework. That's just the beginning and then it gets more complicated [*laughs*] as you go about it.

Billington: That's exactly what I wanted to get into. . . .
Lee: Yeah, what if he wants to hide, what is this, what is that, what if the second story is real, what if the first is partially real, and what if both of them end up bullshitting? However people take it, it has to work at the end. How is the actor going to deliver it so everybody can find that trace? That's a long story, but to me, cinematically, it's a hard one.

Billington: How do you know what from the book you needed to include? How do you know what you can throw out and change but still keep the spirit of the character of Pi?
Lee: Well, gut feeling. Gut feeling in terms of scene, to scene, to scene what it means most is what the book is about—what kind of takes I got and how I want to give that take to the audience cinematically. That first. Then I go about selecting my scenes—what will work for the end. It's pretty much everything to the end. And then I have to choreograph the thing. If I go about the book it will take fifteen hours to play the movie. Can't do that. And the first part of the movie, as you know, it's probably harder to get through. Every aspect of his life, there is a character. There is a math teacher who is the atheist. . . . Everything has a character. You cannot go about that. So I have to consolidate it. I come up with all the atheists go to the father. . . .

Same way with the voyage. Whatever will give a clear storyline that he goes through different stages. We cannot go about things here and there throughout this movie. It has to have some flow. Movie kills a lot quicker once people get an idea they want to move on. So how do you consolidate and pick the best, and the most visualized, too? And there are things I added, like the whale. It's not in the book. But if I want him to lose something, all his belongings, the supplies, I wanted to make it the most magnificent, because Pi's story has to be magnificent. So I came up with ideas like that. And [in the book] the island goes on forever [*laughs*], for maybe months. I have to shrink it down to one day.

Billington: It seems tough to be able to tell a story that can appeal to a wide audience; appeal to atheists as well as Christians, as well as Hindus and so on. Was it tough to find the balance between that without alienating the audience?

Lee: I feel at different phases that's not really a problem. But it's hard to balance the faithful and the atheist. The first thing I talked about, because there are organized religions in the beginning—that's his childhood thing. Then he went through a period he lost the illusion of paradise, the zoo, so to speak. Then he went existential. Then he gets cast away to the ocean to face the abstract idea of God. And that's the real test. So whatever religions, wherever you come from, when he faces the idea of God, you are just social worker. [*laughs*] And we talk about faith; the God that we don't know. I think that part is okay. But for atheists, they probably tend to believe in the second story. You have to work something for them. And for the faithful you have to work it out so it's a faithful story.

My idea—anybody who sees the movie has *their* take, and it will work. I think the nature of the two stories demand that kind of result. That's hard. And then there's an art house and the broader audience. That's even harder [to appeal to], to fundamentally make the movie differently. The challenge I need is not a challenge in art house, but it's a very expensive movie. The anticipation is also very high. It has to appeal to be a broader movie. So that I struggled with [that part] the longest.

Billington: Do you think 3D helped achieve the broader appeal? Not only with the idea that it's popular, but what you were saying earlier about adding depth, too.

Lee: I thought so, but it turns out—give or take movie, doesn't matter 2D or 3D. If they like the story, if they invest in or believe in it, that . . . I thought it makes a difference. That's one of the reasons I started. But then, ideally, it's not the main effect. However, I think 3D makes it seem more like you are together with Pi, especially the ocean part. I think in that respect it helped. I think for all audiences, not just for art house or for the broader audience, it's something new. And also, you literally feel like you are there with him. I think that really helped the movie.

I don't think I can make you fall in love with 3D, not in significance, like what the movie means, but just visually to sit through it and go through what Pi goes through. I think that would be pretty impossible in 2D.

Billington: That's why I called it a 3D masterpiece in that it made it easy to become close to Pi, believe in his story and feel what he felt throughout this experience.

Lee: And also, 3D has this thing . . . take the shot when you see the ship sinking. . . .

Billington: Right—that's an amazing shot.

Lee: And so many times I found myself wanting to shoot the shot behind him. I think that's how we imagine us doing things, whether it's in a dream or imagining doing something. It's always—you are involved, but it's also *point of view*. You are seeing something. Unless you see your head you don't see it, but you feel you are there. So it's kind of an over-shoulder and point of view at the same time.

If you are doing 2D it is just an over-shoulder shot. It's not a point of view. It's not subjective. But with 3D, somehow, if you pull the character outside of the screen, he is on your side. And therefore, you are experiencing more, especially the over-the-shoulder shot sometimes, you really feel like you are him, or he is you. That's just one aspect. . . .

Billington: How did you find Suraj Sharma and cast him as Pi Patel? I heard it was a tough process, but he's impressive. By the end of the movie, I believe his journey, it really feels like he's been through those two hundred days on the boat.

Lee: It literally took that long. It's ten months, the same thing as Pi goes through. I found him through regular casting procedural, which is carpeting India high schools. [*laughs*] Do you want this? Do you want to test? We have a handful, maybe two handfuls, of agents we just ask, and we tried out about three thousand kids, I saw their tape. And after three rounds we narrowed it down to twelve, Suraj was one of them. I saw them and tested them in Mumbai.

Suraj stood out right away. Just looking at him, I began to see the movie. It's a very soulful look. He looks like Pi—smart and witty and sort of . . . you know, it's a vibe. I think camera and audience will like him. I just have that feeling. The casting director agreed with me there. And I tested him. I did a scene. I had him tell the first and second stories. And then I give him a situation and make him believe that's a real story that happened to him, like an equation, the mother is his mother, so on and so forth. And he just stayed there, it was heart wrenching. Toward the end he started to cry. It was a great audition piece and the guy never acted before. Toward the end of the take, sure, not only he is the kid, but it feels like you have a movie. It will be hard, but you start to feel you have something to rely on. The movie is all image; like—*that kid is Pi.*

And then he couldn't swim. He could hold his breath for fifteen seconds. [*laughs*] So, intense physical training, swimming, working out. Physical. He has to get used to water. Boat work, sea legs. I had him take serious yoga lessons just to transform him. Because a lot of acting lessons took from yoga. And I gave him personal acting lessons outside of yoga. A lot of reading materials, watching. . . . And also participating in part of preparation. Every shooting day over five or six months there are training days. And we shoot in water, which is very unusual for a movie this size with these kinds of difficulties. It's miraculous that for the last three months every shot is him and we shoot in water.

If he gets sick, if he gets injured, we don't have a movie, or if he melts down or gets cranky, we are screwed. But every day he is available. And that itself is like a journey. And the last month or so he is getting to this weird insane kind of spiritual, mental place. And I forbid anybody to talk to him. He has to live in silence and only listen to the music I gave him. That was spiritual. And his eyes, you just see him change.

Billington: That's what I mean. You really did put him through the complete experience in the movie.

Lee: And he has to lose weight. So lunchtime is crunch time. He did that for two and a half months, just to gradually lose weight. So everything sort of worked together. It doesn't feel like acting even though he is acting. It's quite unusual. I've done movies for twenty years. This is pretty unusual, I would say.

Billington: Yeah. But that's why I love seeing it. I think it works great and makes for a more honest, genuine performance. But you are almost saying it's not a performance, in a way.

Lee: In some ways that's what acting is about. An experienced actor, regardless of what they have to go through to act like that, they have that innocence, the genuineness. But for him he probably doesn't know that film is not made this way normally. [*laughs*]

Billington: What were the biggest challenges you didn't think would be challenges? And what worked out easier that you thought would be harder?

Lee: Well, kids. Of course we got lucky. It turns out they were the easiest. Tiger, second. It turned out they were great. Not only . . . Some of the shots made it into the movie—we have four tigers. But what we shot of the [real] tiger become good references for [CGI] animation. That's why they behave like tigers. People are saying they couldn't tell the difference.

Billington: Yea, I couldn't either.

Lee: That's the main reason, because we shot endless videos of how tigers behave. We really learned from the tiger. So it was easier than I expected.

Harder—water is harder. 3D is mixed. It's less of a deal than I thought and in some aspects it's bigger of a deal. So it's got plus and minus. But water, it's always . . . however you prepare it, however you expect it, it is always harder than you can prepare, like really hard.

Billington: It's uncontrollable, right?

Lee: Yeah. You just feel helpless.

Billington: You've had a very diverse, very exciting career that continuously progresses in fascinating, brilliant ways. How do you continue to keep yourself evolving as a filmmaker? Where do you see yourself going from here, and how do you choose the stories you make as movies?

Lee: After *Sense and Sensibility*, the first four movies were about the same tone, that was just scary if I kept doing that. I'd reach the end pretty soon. . . . Plus, I think I'm an avid filmmaker. I'm just curious to explore all kinds of filmmaking, all kinds of genres and types of people. Like in *Sense and Sensibility*, the English have certain ways of doing things. A Hong Kong martial arts choreographer, the most brilliant filmmaker, there's always something you'll learn. And when you do Western where it's about boys with guns and horseback. There's always something that made me fascinated.

So, I think I'm just an avid filmmaker. [*laughs*] I'm curious. I don't have a lot of life experience. Growing up I never had much fun. So I just want to make different movies and go to different places. There's a certain center, the core, of me that I cannot avoid. When you make movies sincerely there's always something about you that doesn't change that much.

In terms of material, well that's the part that hits me. When I read some material that hits me at the gut level, but on the surface it has nothing to do with me, it's a strange place that if I have a lot of curiosity, I might fall for it. 'Cause making movies is my life. That's how I want to live my life for the next year or two. . . . I have to dig it, otherwise I cannot convince people around me to follow along with me.

Ang Lee Interview: How He Filmed the Unfilmable for *Life of Pi*

John Hiscock / 2012

From the *Telegraph*, December 19, 2012. © Telegraph Media Group Limited 2012. Reprinted by permission.

It took Ang Lee two months of deep thought before he agreed to take on the job of directing *Life of Pi*, the film version of Yann Martel's Mann Booker Prize–winning novel about a boy and a Bengal tiger marooned on a boat for 227 days.

He knew he would not only be defying the old showbiz adage of never working with children or animals, but there were plenty of other potential problems to consider.

"Kid, water, big special effects, animals—and they have to be in a small boat on water. It seemed to be a filmmaker's every nightmare," he says now. "I thought it was difficult and challenging and I got geared up and decided 'I'll be the one to do this,' but once I got into it I thought it was a dumb idea to have picked it up."

The Oscar-winning director has never been afraid to make difficult choices, and has tackled subjects ranging from a Jane Austen novel (*Sense and Sensibility*) to a love story of two cowboys (*Brokeback Mountain*) and an iconic American rock festival (*Taking Woodstock*).

Even so, the story of an Indian boy on a literal and spiritual journey with a tiger named Richard Parker, a story open to many interpretations, had long been thought to be unfilmable. Other directors, including M. Night Shyamalan and Alfonso Cuaron, had considered and rejected the complex story since Fox acquired the film rights in 2003.

Lee, fifty-eight, took on the project four years ago and almost immediately decided it should be in 3D. "I thought if I did it in another dimension, maybe it would work," he says. "I wanted the experience of the film to be as unique as the book and that meant creating the film in another dimension. 3D is a new cinematic language, and no one really takes it as an art form yet.

"It was a lot harder than I expected. It's a big movie and it was quite tortuous. But I thought it was a calling, something challenging that could be wonderful."

The softly spoken Lee, who has lived in the US for more than thirty years, talks in lengthy, often fractured sentences, smiling frequently and exuding calmness and tranquility, although he acknowledges: "Sometimes I lose my temper. We have so many hundreds of people working so hard for so long during shooting time and you're waiting to capture the moment and the camera's rolling and if anybody is not paying full attention, I will lose it. But even then, not very often. Just a few times on the set."

Lee spent a year preparing the movie and testing ways of animating the tiger before he even cast his star, Suraj Sharma, a seventeen-year-old student and acting newcomer who was discovered after an extensive talent search across India during which more than three thousand young men auditioned. His parents happen to be mathematicians, which prompted Lee to comment: "What are the chances that two mathematicians give birth to a kid who plays the lead in a film called *Life of Pi*?"

Much of the movie was filmed in the world's largest self-generating wave tank, built in Taiwan on the site of a former airport. Lee says: "We got really lucky with the kid. He's in every shot. Very difficult shooting. He never melted down, never got sick, never misbehaved, never got injured. He carried the whole thing. It was a big investment for the studio. Without the kid you are not going to make the movie. And we were lucky with the tiger, too."

Four tigers were used to capture the essence of the ferocious Richard Parker, but for most of the scenes on the boat the tiger was computer-generated.

The movie's story is framed by an author interviewing an older Pi about his experiences. Tobey Maguire, who previously starred in Lee's first American movie, *The Ice Storm*, was cast as the author but after he filmed the role, Lee decided the actor was too famous among a group of relative unknowns, so he recast the British actor Rafe Spall and reshot the sequences.

"It turned out I underestimated how big a movie star Tobey is so I had to redo it," he explained.

Ever since Lee gained international attention with his second feature, *The Wedding Banquet*, in 1993, about a gay Taiwanese man who marries to please his parents, his films have defied pigeonholing. Actors and critics alike have wondered how the director managed to make such varied movies as *Sense and Sensibility*, *Hulk*, *Crouching Tiger, Hidden Dragon*, *Brokeback Mountain* (for which he won the best directing Oscar), and *Taking Woodstock*.

"I never make movies because I'm doing a job; I do them because I'm doing something I like," he explains. "I pick things I have a visceral response to because they have to move me, otherwise there's no point in doing them.

"It's better if I'm not familiar with the material. I had nothing in common with Wyoming gay cowboys but I remember reading the *Brokeback Mountain* short story and I was in tears at the end, which is a good sign.

"I read *Life of Pi* when it first came out and I was fascinated by it—but I didn't think it was a movie."

After Lee's paternal grandparents were executed for being landowners during the Cultural Revolution in China, his father, a scholar and school headmaster, fled to Taiwan, where Ang was born. He studied acting in Taipei before moving to the US, where he attended college at the University of Illinois and then began his moviemaking career at New York University film school.

"I was a very docile, extremely shy and timid kid," he recalls. "I was never rebellious and never lost my composure, but my mind was somewhere else so I was like a spaced-out kid. But once I got to be in touch with art and acted on stage for the first time when I was eighteen, I knew that was what I wanted to do."

Short films he made earned him an agent, but he spent five years struggling to get projects off the ground. During that time he looked after his two sons while his wife, microbiologist Janice Lin, was the family breadwinner.

In 1991, he made his first full-length feature, *Pushing Hands*, from his own screenplay, and followed it with *The Wedding Banquet* and *Eat Drink Man Woman*, all of which gathered critical praise, numerous award nominations and opened the door to Hollywood for him.

He picks his projects carefully and takes his time over them, which is indicated by the fact he has made only twelve full-length feature films in twenty years.

"I'm a slave to a project, not the master," he says. "I'll do whatever it takes to bring it to fruition and make the people who surround me believe in it.

"That is my life for one or two years on a movie, and in the case of *Life of Pi*, nearly four years."

Key Resources

Pushing Hands

Lowenstein, Stephen. "Ang Lee's *Pushing Hands*." *My First Movie*. Ed. Stephen Lowenstein. New York: Pantheon, 2000. 361–81.

The Wedding Banquet

Berry, Chris. "Taiwanese Melodrama Returns with a Twist in the *Wedding Banquet*." *Cinemaya* no. 21 (October 1993): 52–54.

Berry, Chris. "The New Face of Taiwanese Cinema: An Interview with Ang Lee." *Metro*, no. 96, (December 1993): 40–41.

Horn, Andrew. "*The Wedding Banquet*." *Screen International*, no. 897 (March 5, 1993): 22.

Lee, Ang, and Tony Chan. "Dinner for Two." *Filmmaker* 1, no. 4 (July 1993): 22–23.

Leung, William. "So Queer Yet So Straight: Ang Lee's *The Wedding Banquet* and *Brokeback Mountain*." *Journal of Film and Video* 60, no. 1 (April 2008): 23–42.

Spines, Christine. "Indie Jones." *Premiere* 6, no. 12 (August 1993): 51.

Eat Drink Man Woman

Byrge, Duane. "*Eat Drink Man Woman*." *Hollywood Reporter* 332, no. 14 (May 17, 1994): 7, 14.

Comer, Brooke. "*Eat Drink Man Woman*: A Feast for the Eyes." *American Cinematographer* 76, no. 1 (January 1995): 62–67.

Dawes, Amy. "Lee Eats, Drinks, Sleeps Films." *Moving Pictures International*, no. 191 (June 30, 1994): 15.

Errigo, Angie. "New Films." *Empire*, no. 68 (February 1995): 31.

Nathan, Ian. "Global Village: Independent, Foreign, Arthouse: Ang Lee." *Empire*, no. 68 (February 1995): 48–49.

Sense and Sensibility

Cramer, Barbara. "Film Reviews." *Films in Review* 47, no. 3/4 (March 1996): 65–66.

Farrow, Boyd. "Reviews." *Screen International*, no. 1039 (January 1996): 26.

Finnane, Gabriel. "Remarks on Jane Austen and the Period Film." *Metro*, no. 106 (July 1996): 4–12.

Fuller, Graham. "Shtick and Seduction." *Sight and Sound* 6, no. 3 (March 1996): 24.

Fuller, Graham. "Cautionary Tale." *Sight and Sound* 6, no. 3 (March 1996): 20–22.

Gant, Charles. "The Numbers: Austen Power." *Sight and Sound* 15, no. 11 (November 2005): 8.

Geraghty, Christine. "Crossing Over: Performing as a Lady and a Dame." *Screen* 43, no. 1 (April 2002): 41–56.

Gray, Beverly. "Sense & Sensibility: A Script Review." *Creative Screenwriting* 4, no. 2 (July 1997): 74–82.

Hendrickson, Nancy. "License & Liability: Collaborating with Jane Austen." *Creative Screenwriting* 4, no. 2 (July 1997): 62–73.

Leung, William. "Crouching Sensibility, Hidden Sense." *Film Criticism* 26, no. 1 (October 2001): 42–55.

Lyons, Donald. "Passionate Precision." *Film Comment* 32, no. 1 (January 1996): 36–41.

McFarlane, Brian. "Verbal Concepts, Moving Images." *Cinema Papers*, no. 110 (June 1996): 30–32, 60.

Medhurst, Andy: "Dressing the Part." *Sight and Sound* 6, no. 6 (June 1996): 28–30.

Monk, Claire. "Reviews." *Sight and Sound* 6, no. 3 (March 1996): 50–51.

Nathan, Ian. "Front Desk Clips: Hugh's a Clever Boy." *Empire*, no. 81 (March 1996): 17.

Welsh, Jim. "A Sensible Screenplay." *Literature/Film Quarterly* 24, no. 1 (January 1996): 111–12.

The Ice Storm

Aston, Martin. "New Films." *Neon*, February 1998, 86.

Blair, Iain. "Ang Lee." *Film and Video* 13, no. 10 (October 1997): 48–50, 59.

Byrge, Duane. "Film Review." *The Hollywood Reporter* 347, no. 23 (May 1997): 7, 14.

Cheshire, Godfrey. "The Morning After." *Filmmaker* 6, no. 1 (September 1997): 42–43, 89.

David, Andrew. "DVD reviews: The Ice Storm." *Film International* 7, no. 3 (May 2009): 70–71.

Dean, Joan. "American Letter: The '70s, The Way We . . . Weren't." *Film West*, no. 31 (January 1998): 18–19.

Errigo, Angie. New Films." *Empire*, no. 105 (March 1998): 41.

Fisher, Bob. "Fred Elmes, ASC." *Film and Video* 13, no. 10 (October 1997): 59.

Flynn, Bob. "People: Ang Lee / Reviews." *Total Film*, no. 14 (March 1998): 25, 86.

Francke, Lizzie. "Reviews." *Sight and Sound* 8, no. 2 (February 1998): 42.

Fuller, Graham. "Chistina Ricci." *Interview*, October 1997, 102–7, 143.

Fuller, Graham. "Three Films That Show How Frozen We Are." *Interview*, January 1998, 40.

Handelman, David. "Cheat Drink Man Woman." *Premiere* 11, no. 3 (November 1997): 98–115.

Hardesty, Mary. "Ang Lee on Directing in an Ice Storm." *DGA* (Los Angeles), September 1997.

Hemblade, Christopher. "Profiles: Joan Allen." *Empire*, no. 105 (March 1998): 59.

Hunter, Allan. "Cannes Reviews." *Screen International*, no. 1109 (May 1997): 18.

Kirwan, Catherine. "*The Ice Storm.*" *Film Ireland*, no. 63 (February 1998): 39–40.

McCarthy, Todd. "Film Reviews." *Variety*, May 1997, 49, 50.

Moverman, Oren. "The Angle on Ang Lee." *Interview*, September 1997, 64–68.

Westbrook, Caroline. "Front Desk Clips: Tobey Maguire." *Empire*, no. 105 (March 1998): 30.

Williams, David E. "Reflections on an Era." *American Cinematographer* 78, no. 10 (October 1997): 56–58, 60, 62, 64–65.

Ride with the Devil

Bankston, Douglas. "A Less-than-Civil War."*American Cinematographer* 80, no. 11 (November 1999): 66–75.

Calcutt, Ian. "Ride with the Devil." *Film Review*, December 1999, 33.

Collins, Andrew. "Films." *Radio Times*, November 2004, 53.

Eimer, David. "In Person: Tobey Maguire." *Empire*, no. 126 (December 1999): 80–81.

Fuller, Graham. "Reviews: Riders on the Storm." *Sight and Sound* 20, no. 6 (June 2010): 92.

Goodridge, Mike. "*Ride with the Devil.*" *Screen International*, no. 1229 (October 8, 1999): 50.

Kaufman, Anthony. "Cinema Scope review." *Cinema Scope*, no. 1 (September 1999): 30.

Kenny, Glenn. "*Ride with the Devil.*" *Premiere* 13, no. 3 (November 1999): 34.

Matthews, Peter. "Reviews." *Sight and Sound* 9, no. 12 (December 1999): 34–35, 56.

McCarthy, Todd. "Film Reviews." *Variety*, September 13, 1999, 42–43.

Nathan, Ian. "New Films." *Empire*, no. 126 (December 1999): 20–21.

Pinsker, Beth. "The Americanization of Lee: Ang Lee's *Ride with the Devil.*" *Iff (International Film Festival Magazine)*, no. 9 (July 1999): 20–21.

Schwarzbaum, Lisa. "Civil Inaction." *Entertainment Weekly*, no. 515 (December 1999): 73.

Thomson, David. "Riding with Ang Lee." *Film Comment* 35, no. 6 (November 1999): 4–6, 8–9.

Tibbetts, John C. "The Hard Ride: Jayhawkers and Bushwhackers in the Kansas-Missouri Border Wars—*Ride with the Devil.*" *Literature/Film Quarterly* 27, no. 3 (November 1999): 189–95.

Crouching Tiger, Hidden Dragon (Wo Hu Chang Long)

Arnold, Darren. "Crouching Tiger, Hidden Influences." *Metro*, no. 129/130 (December 2001): 180–86.

Brown, Colin. "Crouching Tiger's Hidden Truth." *Screen International*, no. 1296 (February 16, 2001): 26.

Caro, Jason. "*Crouching Tiger, Hidden Dragon.*" *Film Review*, no. 602 (February 2001): 20–21.

Catania, John. "Enter the (Diaspora) Dragons: Martial Arts Cinema and Globalization." *Metro*, no. 148 (April 2006): 96–99.

Chan, Kenneth. "The Global Return of the Wu Xia Pian (Chinese Sword-Fighting Movie): Ang Lee's *Crouching Tiger, Hidden Dragon.*" *Cinema Journal* 43, no. 4 (July 2004): 3–17.

"Chasing the Dragon." *Film Review*, no. 600 (December 2000): 60–61.

"Chinese Whispers." *Film Review*, no. 33 (December 2000): 58–61.

Chute, David. "Year of the Dragon." *Premiere* 14, no. 4 (December 2000): 76–79.

Collins, Andrew. "The Reel Story Behind . . . *Crouching Tiger, Hidden Dragon.*" *Radio Times* 312, no. 4067 (February 16, 2002): 59.

"*Crouching Tiger, Hidden Dragon.*" *Fade In* 6, no. 2 (December 2000): 8–9.

"*Crouching Tiger, Hidden Dragon.*" *Premiere* 14, no. 1 (September 2000): 54.

Dahan, Yannick. "Tigre et dragon: la jeune femme et l'épée." *Positif*, no. 476 (October 2000): 43–44.

Delorme, Gérard. "Tigre et Dragon." *Premiere*, no. 283 (October 2000): 69.

Frater, Patrick. "Chasing the Dragon." *Screen International*, no. 1421 (September 19, 2003): 27, 29.

Freer, Ian. "Remote Control: Soundtracks." *Empire*, no. 141 (March 2001): 140.

Freer, Ian. "'All the Script Said Was, 'They Fight.'" *Empire*, no. 140 (February 2001): 81–83.

Fuller, Graham. "Ang Lee." *Interview*, December 2000, 48, 50, 143.

Gopalan, Nisha. "In the Works: Lee Eyes the 'Tiger.'" *Premiere* 13, no. 4 (December 1999): 34.

Hsiung-Ping, Peggy Chiao. "Chinese Cinema: 1999–2000: Four Traditions, Four Masterpieces."*Cinemaya*, no. 51 (April 2001): 4–12.

Jones, Alan. "Martial Arts Masterpiece." *Cinefantastique* 32, no. 6 (February 2001): 7.

Kabir, Nasreen Munni, et al. "*Crouching Tiger Hidden Dragon.*" *Vertigo* 2, no. 1 (April 2001): 6–9.

Kane, Stephen. "Crouching Tiger, Oscar Runner." *Film Ireland*, no. 79 (February 2001): 16–18.

Kaufman, Anthony. "Cannes 2000: Ang-tastic!: *Crouching Tiger, Hidden Dragon*." *Cinema Scope*, no. 4 (July 2000): 42–43.

Kemp, Philip. "Stealth and Duty." *Sight and Sound* 10, no. 12 (December 2000): 12–15.

Kenny, Glenn. "*Crouching Tiger, Hidden Dragon*." *Premiere* 14, no. 5 (January 2001): 21–22.

Klein, Christina. "*Crouching Tiger, Hidden Dragon*: A Diasporic Reading." *Cinema Journal* 43, no. 4 (July 2004): 18–42.

Lin, Frank. "Searching for the Hidden Dragon: An Evening with Ang Lee." *The Directors Guild of America Magazine* 25, no. 6 (March 2001): 17–20.

Loiseau, Jean-Claude. "Tigre et Dragon." *Télérama*, no. 2647 (October 7, 2000): 60–61.

Loiseau, Jean-Claude. "Ang Lee Terrasse le Dragon." *Télérama*, no. 2647 (October 7, 2000): 56–57.

Lyman, Peter. "Watching Movies with Ang Lee: Crouching Memory, Hidden Heart." *New York Times*, March 9, 2001, E1, E27.

Magid, Ron. "High-Wire Act." *American Cinematographer* 82, no. 1 (January 2001): 64–65.

Malcolm, Derek. "Cannes Reviews: *Crouching Tiger, Hidden Dragon*." *Screen International*, no. 1260 (May 2000): 19.

McCarthy, Todd. "Film Reviews." *Variety*, May 22, 2000, 19, 32.

"Michelle Yeoh." *Premiere*, no. 283 (October 2000): 111.

Nathan, Ian. "New Films." *Empire*, no. 140 (February 2001): 38.

Nordin, Kenneth D. "Shadow Archetypes in Ang Lee's *Crouching Tiger, Hidden Dragon* and *The Hulk*: A Jungian Perspective." *Asian Cinema* 15, no. 2 (December 2004): 120–32.

Norman, Barry. "Tiger Burning Bright." *Radio Times* 308, no. 4010 (January 9, 2001): 49.

Persons, Mitch. "Ang Lee on *Crouching Tiger, Hidden Dragon*." *Cinefantastique* 33, no. 1/2 (April 2001): 96–99.

Pham, Minh-Ha T. "The Asian Invasion (of Multiculturalism) in Hollywood." *Journal of Popular Film & Television* 32, no. 3 (October 2004): 121–31.

Piegay, Baptiste. "Retour en Asie." *Cahiers du Cinéma*, no. 550 (October 2000): 102–3.

Pizzello, Chris. "DVD Playback." *American Cinematographer* 82, no. 8 (August 2001): 14.

Rayns, Tony. "Reviews." *Sight and Sound* 11, no. 1 (January 2001): 45–46.

Roddick, Nick. "Rushes: Uncertain Regard: No More Auteurs Anymore." *Sight and Sound* 11, no. 1 (January 2001): 5.

Roman, Shari. "Lifestyles of the Bitchin' Schamus." *Fade In* 6, no. 3 (May 2001): 56–57.

Roman, Shari. "Master Lee." *Fade In* 6, no. 2 (December 2000): 20–21.

Rynning, Roald, and James Mottram. "Ang Tough." *Film Review*, no. 602 (February 2001): 50–54.

S. D. "'Tigre et dragon' griffe les cinéphiles et les femmes." *Le Film Francais*, no. 2846 (September 8, 2000): 27.

Schamus, James. "Aesthetic Identities: A Response to Kenneth Chan and Christina Klein." *Cinema Journal* 43, no. 4 (July 2004): 43–52.

Seguin, Denis. "Tiger Claws at Subtitle Barrier." *Screen International*, no. 1292 (January 19, 2001): 1, 4.

Stephens, Chuck. "*Crouching Tiger, Hidden Dragon*." *Film Comment* 36, no. 6 (November 2000): 73.

"Tigre et Dragon." *L'Avant-Scène du Cinéma*, no. 502 (May 2001): [whole issue].

Walsh, Mike, and Peter Gravestock. "The Good Fight: An Interview with Zheng Pei-pei." *Metro*, no. 138 (October 2003): 118–20.

Weitzman, Elizabeth. "Zhang Ziyi." *Interview*, December 2000, 52–53.

Williams, David E. "Images for the Ages." *American Cinematographer* 82, no. 6 (June 2001):100–102.

Williams, David E. "Enter the Dragon." *American Cinematographer* 82, no. 1 (January 2001): 68–77.

Williams, David E. "High-Flying Adventure." *American Cinematographer* 82, no. 1 (January 2001): 54–62, 66–67.

Wu, Chia-Chi. "*Crouching Tiger, Hidden Dragon* Is Not a Chinese Film." *Spectator* 22 no. 1, (April 2002): 65–79.

Yu, Shu Lien. "January: *Crouching Tiger, Hidden Dragon*." *StarBurst*, no. 50 (December 2001): 6–7.

"Zhang Ziyi." *Premiere*, no. 283 (October 2000): 110.

Hulk

Bankston, Douglas. "Jolly Green Giant." *Cinefantastique* 35, no. 4 (August 2003): 62.

Braund, Simon. "The Reviews." *Empire*, no. 170 (August 2003): 42–43.

Dinning, Mark, and Helen O'Hara. "Movie Trial: *Hulk*." *Empire*, no. 215 (May 2007): 160–61.

Flanagan, Martin. "*The Hulk*, an Ang Lee Film." *New Review of Film and Television* 2, no. 1 (May 2004): 19–35.

Fordham, Joe. "Green Destiny." *Cinefex*, no. 94 (July 2003): 74–126.

France, Michael. "Letters: Hulking Issues."*Cinefantastique* 35, no. 4 (August 2003): 79.

Goodridge, Mike. "What Has Gone Wrong in the US?" *Screen International*, no. 1412 (July 11, 2003): 1–2.

Grey, Ian. "An Even More Incredible Hulk." *Fangoria*, no. 223 (June 2003): 46–49, 82.

Gross, Edward, Kevin H. Martin, and Gina McIntyre. "Anger Management." *Cinefan-tastique* 35, no. 3 (June 2003): 24–36.

Gross, Edward. "A Film without Fear." *Cinefantastique* 35, no. 1 (February 2003): 30–49.

Jauberty, Christian. "Banaboum!" *Premiere*, no. 317 (July 2003): 76–79.

Jauberty, Christian. "Cahier Critique." *Premiere*, no. 317 (July 2003): 28.

Kay, Jeremy. "People: Green Energy." *Screen International*, no. 1649 (June 27, 2008): 8.

Kempster, Grant. "Smoke and Mirrors." *StarBurst* v.Spec, no. 61 (December 2003): 28–35.

Magid, Ron. "Growing Pains." *American Cinematographer* 84, no. 7 (July 2003): 46–57.

Magid, Ron. "A Spectacular Virtual Vista." *American Cinematographer* 84, no. 7 (July 2003): 54–55.

McCarthy, Todd. "Film Reviews." *Variety*, June 16, 2003, 25, 32.

Mitchell, Peter. "It Ain't Easy Being Green." *Inside Film*, no. 56 (July 2003): 38–39, 41.

Narbonne, Christophe. "Cahier Critique." *Premiere*, no. 317 (July 2003): 28.

Norman, Barry. "Barry Norman on Ang Lee." *Radio Times*, April 17, 2004, 47.

O'Brien, Geoffrey. "Something's Gotta Give." *Film Comment* 39, no. 4 (July 2003): 28–30.

Perenson, Melissa. "Hulk." *StarBurst*, no. 300 (June 2003): 82–89.

Perenson, Melissa J. "Brute Strength." *StarBurst*, no. 299 (May 2003): 54–57.

Roston, Tom. "ID Could Happen to You." *Premiere* 16, no. 11 (July 2003): 86–90, 119.

Sloane, Judy. "Hulk." *StarBurst*, no. 58 (July 2003): 33–38.

Smith, Adam. "The Beast Within." *Empire*, no. 169 (July 2003): 66–77.

"Summer Movie Preview." *Premiere* 16, no. 10 (June 2003): 68.

Switzer, Sara. "Mike Erwin." *Interview*, July 2003, 18.

White, Rob. "Reviews: the Main Attraction." *Sight and Sound* 13, no. 8 (August 2003): 34–35, 46–47.

Williams, David E. "Temper, Temper: Director of Photography Frederick Elmes, ASC Lends Dramatic Moods to *The Hulk*, the Big-Screen Debut of a Very Angry Super-hero." *American Cinematographer* 84, no. 7 (July 2003): 34–45.

Wood, Aylish. "Encounters at the Interface: Distributed Attention and Digital Em-bodiments." *Quarterly Review of Film and Video* 25, no. 3 (May 2008): 219–29.

Wood, Aylish. "Pixel Visions: Digital Intermediates and Micromanipulations of the Image." *Film Criticism* 32, no. 1 (October 2007): 72–94.

Brokeback Mountain

"Acting Up." *Premiere* 19, no. 5 (February 2006): 82–96.

Berry, Chris. "The Chinese Side of the Mountain." *Film Quarterly* 60, no. 3 (April 2007): 32–37.

Bowen, Peter. "The Other Side of the Mountain." *Screen International*, no. 1552 (June 16, 2006): 4–5.

Bowen, Peter. "Ride the High Country." *Filmmaker* 14, no. 1 (October 2005): 34–39.

Brett, Anwar. "East Meets Western." *Film Review*, no. 665 (January 2006): 56–59.

Brower, Sue. "'They'd Kill Us if They Knew': Transgression and the Western." *Journal of Film and Video* 62, no. 4 (December 2010): 47–57.

Calhoun, John. "Peaks and Valleys." *American Cinematographer* 87, no. 1 (January 2006): 58–60, 62–64, 67.

Clarke, Roger. "Lonesome Cowboys." *Sight and Sound* 16, no. 1 (January 2006): 28–33.

Clover, Joshua, and Christopher Nealon. "Don't Ask, Don't Tell Me." *Film Quarterly* 60, no. 3 (April 2007): 62–67.

Collins, Andrew. "The Celluloid Closet." *Radio Times*, May 17, 2008, 49.

Edgecombe, Rodney Stenning. "The Formal Design of *Brokeback Mountain*." *Film Criticism* 31, no. 3 (April 2007): 2–14.

Evans, Alex. "How Homo Can Hollywood Be? Remaking Queer Authenticity from *To Wong Foo* to *Brokeback Mountain*." *Journal of Film and Video* 61, no. 4 (December 2009): 41–54.

Fuller, Graham. "Michelle Williams." *Interview*, March 2006, 160–67.

Gant, Charles. "Going for *Brokeback*." *Sight and Sound* 16, no. 3 (March 2006): 8.

Gilbey, Ryan. "*Brokeback Mountain*." *Sight and Sound* 16, no. 1 (January 2006): 50.

Goodridge, Mike. "Women on Top." *Screen International*, no. 1528 (December 16, 2005): 18–21.

Goodridge, Mike. "A Very Open Race." *Screen International*, no. 1527 (December 9, 2005): 16, 18, 20.

Goodridge, Mike. "Best in the Business." *Screen International*, no. 1526 (December 2, 2005): 14, 16, 18–19.

Greven, David. "Contemporary Hollywood Masculinity and the Double-Protagonist Film." *Cinema Journal* 48, no. 4 (July 2009): 22–43.

Jones, Anderson. "The Other Side of the Mountain." *Fade In* 9, no. 1 (January 2006): 22–23.

Jones, Alan. "*Brokeback Mountain*." *Film Review*, no. 665 (January 2006): 104–5.

Kenny, Glenn. "*Brokeback Mountain*." *Premiere* 19, no. 4 (December 2005): 52, 56.

Kitses, Jim. "All That Brokeback Allows." *Film Quarterly* 60, no. 3 (April 2007): 22–27.

Lim, Song Hwee. "Is the Trans-in Transnational the Trans-in Transgender?" *New Cinemas Journal of Contemporary Film* 5, no. 1 (May 2007): 39–52.

Macnab, Geoffrey. "*Brokeback Mountain*." *Sight and Sound* 16, no. 7 (July 2006): 86–87.

McCarthy, Todd. "Film Reviews." *Variety*, September 12, 2005, 63.

Miller, D. A. "On the Universality of *Brokeback*." *Film Quarterly* 60, no. 3 (April 2007): 50–60.

Mottram, James. "Full Metal Jake." *Film Review*, no. 666 (February 2006): 48–53.

Norman, Barry. "Barry Norman's Greatest Hits." *Radio Times*, September 13, 2008, 44.

Osterweil, Ara. "Ang Lee's Lonesome Cowboys." *Film Quarterly* 60, no. 3 (April 2007): 38–42.

Prince, Chris. "*Brokeback Mountain*." *Film Review*, no. 670 (June 2006): 112.

Rich, B. Ruby. "Brokering *Brokeback*: Jokes, Backlashes and Other Anxieties." *Film Quarterly* 60, no. 3 (April 2007): 44–48.

Rosen, Lisa. "Go Tell It on the Mountain." *Written By* 10, no. 1 (January 2006): 26–31, 50, 52.

Sharrett, Christopher. "Death of the Strong, Silent Type: The Achievements of *Brokeback Mountain*." *Film International* 7, no. 1 (January 2009): 16–27.

Smith, Adam. "The Searchers." *Empire*, no. 199 (January 2006): 120–22, 125.

Spohrer, Erika. "Not a Gay Cowboy Movie? *Brokeback Mountain* and the Importance of Genre." *Journal of Popular Film & Television* 37, no. 1 (April 2009): 26–33.

Wharton, David Michael. "*Brokeback Mountain*: Screenplay by Larry McMurtry and Diana Ossana." *Creative Screenwriting* 12, no. 6 (November 2005): 24.

Wise, Damon. "In Cinemas: *Brokeback Mountain*." *Empire*, no. 199 (January 2006): 44–45.

Wood, Robin. "On and Around Brokeback Mountain." *Film Quarterly* 60, no. 3 (April 2007): 28–31.

Lust, Caution

"A Lusty Rating for *Caution* (Cover Story)." *Daily Variety* 296, no. 39 (2007): 1–12.

"China Cut an Exercise in *Caution*." *Hollywood Reporter—International Edition* 400, no. 51 (2007): 83.

Davies, Rebecca. "Firestorm." *New Statesman* 137, no. 4878 (2008): 34–36.

Dilley, Whitney Crothers. "Globalization and Cultural Identity in the Films of Ang Lee." *Style* 43, no. 1 (2009): 45–64.

Donald, Stephanie Hemelryk. "Tang Wei." *Theory, Culture & Society* 27, no. 4 (2010): 46–68.

Goldstein, Gregg. "Focus Says It Won't Sweat NC-17 Given to Lee's *Lust*." *Hollywood Reporter—International Edition* 400, no. 48 (2007): 2–51.

Goldstein, Gregg. "Leung, Tang Heeding Lee's *Lust, Caution*." *Hollywood Reporter—International Edition* 395, no. 12 (2006): 4–70.

Hamer, Molly. "Not Notorious Enough: The Transnational Feminism of Ang Lee's *Lust, Caution* and Its American Reception." *Asian Cinema* 22, no. 2 (2011): 322–51.

Hill, Logan. "How Ang Lee Earned His NC-17." *New York* 40, no. 35 (2007): 80–81.

James, Nick. "Cruel Intentions." *Sight and Sound* 18, no. 1 (2008): 47–50.

"Lee Flagging *Caution* for Next Project." *Hollywood Reporter—International Edition* 394, no. 3 1 (2006): 45.

Leung, William. "Sex, China and Propaganda." *Metro* 156 (2008): 50–56.

Morfoot, Addie. "Lee Professes Love for *Lust*." *Daily Variety* 297, no. 2 (2007): 11.

Shen, Vivian. "History, Fiction, and Film—*Lust, Caution* Revisited." *Asian Cinema* 22, no. 2 (2011): 305–21.

Thomson, Patricia. "Emotional Betrayal." *American Cinematographer* (October 2007): 48–54, 56, 58–59.

Wise, Damon. "Censor Sensibility." *Empire*, December 2007, 166–68.

Taking Woodstock

Cieutat, Michel. "Cannes 2009: Notes sur les Films." *Positif*, no. 581/582 (July 2009): 105–6.

Gilbey, Ryan. "Reviews: *Taking Woodstock*." *Sight and Sound* 19, no. 12 (December 2009): 76–77.

Goodridge, Mike. "Awards Countdown: Actors and Actresses." *Screen International*, no. 1713 (December 11, 2009): 14–19.

Hunter, Allan. "Reviews: Cannes: *Taking Woodstock*." *Screen International* no. 1691 (May 29, 2009): 25.

McCarthy, Todd. "Film Reviews." *Variety*, May 25, 2009, 18.

Pierce, Nev. "Re.View: *Taking Woodstock*." *Empire*, no. 249 (March 2010): 149.

Schreiber, Liev. "Love Fest." *Interview* (August 2009): 30–33.

Thomas, William. "The Smoking Hot Preview: *Taking Woodstock*." *Empire*, no. 243 (August 2009): 85.

Wilding, Philip. "In Cinemas: *Taking Woodstock*." *Empire*, no. 246 (December 2009): 70.

Wise, Damon. "Hippie Talking." *Empire*, no. 245 (November 2009): 130–32.

Life of Pi

Baum, Gary. "No Animals Were Harmed." *Hollywood Reporter* 419, no. 43 (2013): 62–78.

Boucher, Geoff. "Ang Lee: *Life of Pi*." *Entertainment Weekly* 1243/1244 (2013): 72.

Breznican, Anthony. "Fall Movie Preview: *Life of Pi*." *Entertainment Weekly* 1220/1221 (2012): 64–66.

Chagollan, Steve. "Ang Lee: *Life of Pi*." *Daily Variety* 318, no. 11 (2013): 12.

Cox, Gordon. "Waiting to Inhale." *Daily Variety* 317, no. 2 (2012): 15.

Essman, Scott. "VFX Team Dares to Take Tiger by the Tail." *Daily Variety* 317, no. 54 (2012): 10.

Fleming, Michael. "Lee Figures into *Pi*." *Daily Variety* 302, no. 33 (2009): 1–17.

Jones, Bill T. "Ang Lee." *Variety* 429, no. 7 (2012): 75.

Konstantinides, Anneta. "3D Org to Fete Lee for *Pi*." *Daily Variety* 317, no. 44 (2012): 2.

Macaulay, Scott. "Editing *Life of Pi*." *Filmmaker: The Magazine of Independent Film* 21, no. 1 (2012): 72–84.

Martin, Kevin H. "Eye of the Tiger." *International Cinematographers Guild Magazine* 83, no. 11 (2012): 48–54.

McClintock, Pamela. "Making of *Life of Pi*." *Hollywood Reporter* 41 (2012): 78–82.

"The Movies Become Him." *Daily Variety* 317, no. 13 (2012): 15.

Vineyard, Jennifer. "He Bought a Zoo." *New York* 45, no. 40 (2012): 82.

Other

"Ang Lee: Director." *ReelWest Magazine*, August 2003.

Berry, Michael. *Speaking in Images*. Columbia University Press, 2005. 324, 361.

Cavagna, Carlo. "Interview: Ang Lee with Carlo Cavagna." AboutFilm.com, December 2006.

Stevens, Andrew. "Interview with Ang Lee." CNN.com/Asia, October 26, 2007. http://www.cnn.com/2007/WORLD/asiapcf/10/08/talkasia.anglee/

Stone, Judy. *Eye on the World: Conversations with International Filmmakers*. Los Angeles: Silman-James Press, 1997.

Index

Made in the USA
Columbia, SC
29 December 2019